Praise for
The Essential Guide f
Beginning English Learners

"*The Essential Guide for Educating Beginning English Learners* is a direct, concise, and straight-forward volume for practitioners serving newly arrived English language learners. It captures the assets and resources beginning ELLs bring into the classroom and focuses on effective educational responses for each group of beginning English learners, built around a solid understanding of key learner characteristics, including literacy levels, cultural characteristics, and other important learner factors that may come into play such as poverty and/or trauma experienced. The authors have created a useful working guide, supported by plenty of helpful examples and tools, which schools can use to facilitate professional development communities, following a structured book study process."

Nancy Cloud, Professor and Director of the MEd in TESL Program
Rhode Island College, Providence, RI

"At a time when the U.S. is experiencing a record number of English learners, this carefully researched, practical guide will serve as the primary support for both teachers and administrators seeking to do a more comprehensive job of responding to what is arguably their most vulnerable student population. Zacarian and Haynes provide a close examination of the diversity within the group of beginner ELs, who are often lumped together based on language proficiency alone."

Helaine W. Marshall, Associate Professor of Education,
Director of Language Education Programs
Long Island University Hudson, Purchase, NY

"Debbie Zacarian and Judie Haynes joined forces again and created a much needed, comprehensive text in *The Essential Guide for Educating Beginning English Learners*. Students who are new to the English language and often new to the United States and the U.S. school system frequently encounter complex challenges, so their teachers need to be prepared and ready to help. This book will serve as an indispensable resource for teachers to tackle this task, and to do so with knowledge, skills, confidence, and advocacy for new English learners!"

Andrea Honigsfeld, Professor
Molloy College

"More than ever, educators are facing large numbers of English learners, each coming with specific needs. The authors present a comprehensive text of how educators can and should work with these students and their families. Many of the strategies presented can be applied to other students as well. This book will be a valuable asset to every educator who wants each of his or her students to succeed."

Glen Ishiwata, Former Superintendent
Moreland School District, San Jose, CA

"This book is a must-read for teachers and administrators. It provides a comprehensive approach to helping EL students learn academic language, which is key to success in the content areas. This book provides an excellent opportunity for leaders as a book study with its guidance and reflections throughout the chapters."

Maria H. Gillentine, Title III Program Specialist
Gwinnett County Public Schools, Suwanee, GA

The Essential Guide for
EDUCATING BEGINNING
ENGLISH LEARNERS

With a combined six decades of experience, we continue to promote the ideals of public education—to help students become active members and successful learners in their school communities and beyond. We dedicate this book to them and their families and to the educators from whom we continue learn so much.

The Essential Guide for
EDUCATING BEGINNING
ENGLISH LEARNERS

Debbie Zacarian ▪ Judie Haynes

San Diego Christian College
2100 Greenfield Drive
El Cajon, CA 92019

CORWIN
A SAGE Company

CORWIN
A SAGE Company

FOR INFORMATION:

Corwin

A SAGE Company

2455 Teller Road

Thousand Oaks, California 91320

(800) 233-9936

www.corwin.com

SAGE Publications Ltd.

1 Oliver's Yard

55 City Road

London EC1Y 1SP

United Kingdom

SAGE Publications India Pvt. Ltd.

B 1/I 1 Mohan Cooperative Industrial Area

Mathura Road, New Delhi 110 044

India

SAGE Publications Asia-Pacific Pte. Ltd.

3 Church Street

#10-04 Samsung Hub

Singapore 049483

Acquisitions Editor: Dan Alpert

Associate Editor: Megan Bedell

Editorial Assistant: Heidi Arndt

Production Editor: Cassandra Margaret Seibel

Copy Editor: Sarah J. Duffy

Typesetter: C&M Digitals (P) Ltd.

Proofreader: Wendy Jo Dymond

Indexer: Jean Casalegno

Cover Designer: Michael Dubowe

Permissions Editor: Karen Ehrmann

Printed in the United States of America.

Library of Congress Cataloging-in-Publication Data

Zacarian, Debbie.

The essential guide for educating beginning English learners / Debbie Zacarian, Judie Haynes.

p. cm.

Includes bibliographical references and index.

ISBN 978-1-4522-2615-6 (pbk.)

1. English language—Study and teaching—United States—Foreign speakers. I. Haynes, Judie. II. Title.

PE1128.A2Z23 2012

428.0071—dc23   2012020442

This book is printed on acid-free paper.

Certified Chain of Custody
SUSTAINABLE Promoting Sustainable Forestry
FORESTRY www.sfiprogram.org
INITIATIVE SFI-01268

SFI label applies to text stock

12 13 14 15 16 10 9 8 7 6 5 4 3 2 1

Contents

Additional materials and resources related to *The Essential Guide for Educating Beginning English Learners* can be found at www.corwin.com/beginningells.

Acknowledgments

This was our second project together and a great experience from start to finish. We could not have done it without the support of many people. Special thanks to

- Dan Alpert, whose outstanding editorial support from inception to the final product was always positive, patient, and encouraging.
- Sara Boyd, from North Kansas City Schools, for sharing her knowledge and stories about students from Africa with limited and interrupted formal education.
- Monica Schnee, from River Edge Public Schools in New Jersey, who informed us about the learning needs of English learner kindergartners entering school in the United States.
- Ken Pransky, from the Collaborative for Educational Services in Northampton, Massachusetts, who expanded our thinking about culturally and linguistically diverse learners—especially those who have experienced cultural disruptions.
- Audrey Morse, also from the Collaborative for Educational Services, whose background as a speech and language pathologist, an ESL teacher, and a teacher educator helped our thinking about English learners with learning differences and disabilities.
- the many classroom teachers, specialists, and school leaders from across the country who graciously shared their work with us.
- the external reviewers of the manuscript whose ideas and suggestions greatly strengthened the book.
- Cassandra Seibel and Sarah Duffy, from Corwin, who polished our writing to make it shine.

We spent many long hours collaborating on the *Essential Guide for Educating Beginning English Learners.* We couldn't have written it without the steadfast encouragement of our families and especially our husbands, Matt Zacarian and Joe Haynes.

PUBLISHER'S ACKNOWLEDGMENTS

Corwin gratefully acknowledges the contributions of the following reviewers:

Torii Bottomley
ESL Teacher and Trainer
Boston Public Schools
Cambridge, MA

Michelle DaCosta
Bilingual Resource Teacher
Framingham Public Schools
Framingham, MA

Glen Ishiwata
Former Superintendent
Moreland School District
San Jose, CA

Katherine Lobo
ESL Teacher and Teacher Trainer
Belmont Public Schools
Belmont, MA

Beth Madison
Principal
George Middle School
Portland, OR

Amy Mares
Coordinator for Bilingual/ESL Instructional Services
Region One Education Service Center
Edinburg, TX

Jen Paul
ELL Assessment Consultant
Michigan Department of Education
Lansing, MI

About the Authors

 **Debbie Zacarian,** EdD has authored numerous publications including *Mastering Academic Language (2013), The Essential Guide for Educating Beginning English Learners* (2012), *Transforming Schools for English Learners: A Comprehensive Framework for School Leaders* (2011), and *Teaching English Language Learners Across the Content Areas* (2010), and was a columnist for TESOL's *Essential Teacher*. A national expert in policies and practices, she cowrote the Massachusetts Department of Early Education and Care's policies for dual language learners; wrote Serving English Learners: Laws, Policies, and Regulations, a user-friendly guide about U.S. federal laws, a project funded with support from the Carnegie Foundation for Colorín Colorado; and served as expert consultant with the Kindergarten Entry Assessment Advisory Committee of the Delaware Governor's Office, Delaware Children's Department, and Delaware's Office of Education. With over three decades of combined experience directing a professional development and consulting center at an educational service agency about English language education and advancing student achievement, administering public school English learner programs, serving on the faculty of the University of Massachusetts Amherst, and engaging in various state and national initiatives, Dr. Zacarian consults with state agencies and school districts in the United States on policies, programming, and professional development for culturally and linguistically diverse populations.

Judie Haynes is a freelance professional development provider and teacher with 28 years' experience in teaching English as a second language. She has published six books, including *Getting Started With English Language Learners* (ASCD, 2007) and *Teaching English language Learners Across the Content Areas* (ASCD, 2010). Judie also contributed chapters to *Integrating the ESL Standards Into Classroom Practice, Grades K–2* (TESOL, 2000) and *Authenticity in the Language Classroom and Beyond* (TESOL, 2010). She was also a columnist for TESOL's *Essential Teacher*. Judie is the editor and owner of everythingESL.net, a website for teachers of English learners. She is cofounder and moderator of #ELLCHAT, an online chat for teachers of English learners. She also provides keynote addresses and workshops to TESOL affiliates and school districts all over the United States.

Introduction

The population of English learners in U.S. public and public charter schools is growing at a rapid and continuous rate. This growth is occurring while the total population remains relatively unchanged. As a result, our schools are becoming more and more populated with English learners (ELs).

Many teachers, administrators, specialists, and other stakeholders are in a quandary about what to do with beginning-level ELs, especially those with no or limited literacy and schooling experiences. They describe this as the most challenging aspect of working with this population.

The Essential Guide for Educating Beginning English Learners focuses on helping administrators, teachers, curriculum supervisors, teacher leaders, teacher educators, and others to prepare for ELs who are at the beginning stages of English language acquisition. This comprises three groups of ELs: those with literacy and school experiences in their home countries that are commensurate with American public schools, those with no or limited prior school experiences, and those who are experiencing the effects of trauma violence. The goal of our book is to help preservice teachers, administrators, and others who are just starting to work with this population, as well as veterans to build a welcoming classroom and school environment where ELs and their families can be engaged and can flourish. Each chapter opens with a scenario and focuses on key elements of teaching beginning ELs.

Chapter 1: Seeing the Big Picture

In Chapter 1, we describe the increase of ELs and discuss their performance in U.S. schools. We provide a rationale for creating optimal learning and school community environments for ELs at the beginning levels of learning English. Our focus on this particular segment of the population is based on the reality that these students are not being provided with programming that is targeted for their needs. Using an asset-based model, we provide a framework for addressing this growing population more effectively.

Chapter 2: Taking a Closer Look

In this chapter, we examine beginning-level ELs through the lens of literacy as well as ELs who have experienced trauma. We elaborate on different types of literacy orientations and describe how different perceptions about time, individualism, and collectivism bear on the school performance of EL. We then discuss the mismatch that can occur between students and their educators. We also discuss the role that cultural disruptions and poverty play in this dynamic. Using an asset-based model, we begin to outline the steps that are needed to improve classroom and school environments.

Chapter 3: Effective Programming for English Learners

This chapter focuses on the key elements that should be included in identifying ELs and creating programming for them. We include a variety of forms and practices to support as seamless an enrollment process as possible and discuss the methods that should be used for identifying ELs and designing instructional programs that support their language, literacy, and academic development.

Chapter 4: Selecting Models of Instruction

In this chapter, we describe the different kinds of programs for ELs and how they affect the education of students who are just beginning to learn English. We include some of the factors that are important to consider in building programming for this group.

Chapter 5: Strengthening Family–School Engagement

This chapter discusses the importance of building partnerships with families of beginning ELs by taking five essential steps—understanding barriers, establishing a welcoming environment by building relationships, addressing differences, building connections with learning, supporting advocacy—all so we can form the foundation for empowering parents as important and critical assets in their child's education.

Chapter 6: Teaching Beginners

This chapter moves students from their first months of school through the beginning stages of learning English. We include a framework for supporting educators to understand how learning English and content is social, developmental, academic, and based on building school-matched thinking skills. We present realistic expectations that teachers should have during this development phase and describe how to build a rich instructional program based on what students can do.

Chapter 7: Working With English Learners Who Have Experienced Trauma

In this chapter, we discuss the trauma (i.e., war, natural disasters, and personal trauma) that some ELs have endured, or are still enduring, and how schools can build "trauma-sensitive" practices while supporting social, language/literacy, academic, and thinking skill development within a whole-school, whole-classroom context.

Chapter 8: Teaching English Learners With Limited or Interrupted Formal Education

In this chapter, we address who students with limited or interrupted formal education are and how schools can adapt programs for them. Using an asset-based model, we focus on programs that support student acquisition of English, literacy, and academic content.

Chapter 9: Providing Effective Professional Development

This chapter is devoted to a detailed description of the types of professional development activities that should occur for preservice and in-service teachers and administrators of beginning ELs. Included are observation, reflection, and interview tasks along with accompanying chapter-by-chapter activities for using this book in professional development settings.

1 Seeing the Big Picture

When Mei moved from Beijing to a small urban city in the northeastern United States, her family gathered her prior school records. With these in hand, they hoped to find someone at the school who would help them enroll their daughter. They waited by the school's front door for someone to let them in. When no one came, they knocked softly and when no one answered, they politely continued to wait. After several minutes, another adult walked to the front door. Instead of knocking on it, they observed that she pressed a button and spoke into an intercom. Shortly afterward, a buzzer sounded and the woman motioned for Mei and her family to enter through the front door with her. They followed the woman to the school office, where they waited several long minutes until the school secretary finally looked at them. Unsure about what to do, they said, "We bring Mei school." In reply, the secretary asked, "Does she speak English?" "Little bit," they replied. "Okay," the secretary said, "we'll have to figure something out." Then, the school's secretary gave Mei 's family a packet of forms to complete. Not sure what the forms were about, the family silently left the school trying to determine who could help them enroll their child. They finally were able to contact a Mandarin-speaking family member to ask for help. A week later the Li family returned the forms to the school only to be told that Mei needed some inoculations. This delayed her school entry by another week. By the time Mei began school, over 2 weeks had transpired.

When the first day of school arrived, Mei's family dropped her off at 7:00 a.m., the time that school started in China. Mei waited outside for over an hour for the doors of the school to open. No one had told her family what time school started. When Mei was finally able to enter the school, she was not sure where to go and was unable to ask. Overall she and her family did not feel welcomed by the school, and that feeling of being outsiders persisted throughout Mei's schooling.

HOW ARE ENGLISH LEARNERS DOING IN U.S. SCHOOLS?

In the United States, English learners (ELs) represent a rapidly growing population. According to the National Center for Education Statistics (2009), the population of ELs increased from 3.8 million to close to 11 million from 1990 to 2009, and these learners represent over 20% of the total population of the nation's students. This growth has occurred while the nation's total population remains relatively unchanged. As a result, while the total student population is not growing, schools are becoming more and more populated with ELs (see Figure 1.1).

WHO ARE BEGINNING ENGLISH LEARNERS?

While many may believe that the growth is due to an increased population of immigrants, most ELs in the nation's schools—close to 75%, in fact—are born in the United States (Capps et al, 2005). The remainder come from many different countries. Additionally, there is sweeping diversity among the nation's ELs, including the reality that there are over 350 languages spoken among them (Capps et al., 2005; Garcia, Jensen, & Scribner, 2009) and the majority live 200% below the poverty level ("A Distinct Population," 2009; Goldenberg & Coleman, 2010). In addition, their public and public

Figure 1.1   Total Enrollment of General Student Population and English Learners

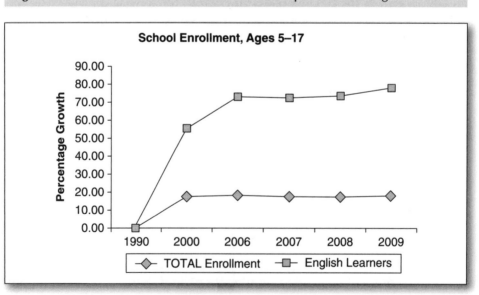

Source: National Center on Educational Statistics.

charter schools experiences widely vary. Over half are attending schools in places where they represent less than 1% of the total EL population (National Center for Education Statistics, 2004). Like Mei, the student presented at the beginning of this chapter, they are enrolling in schools where there are few ELs like themselves and they are being taught by educators with no or limited experience working with this population.

In addition, ELs range in stages of English language development: Level 1: starting, Level 2: emerging, Level 3: developing, Level 4: expanding, and Level 5: bridging and reaching (Teachers of English to Speakers of Other Languages, 1996–2007). In this book, we use the term *beginning ELs* to include students who are at the starting and emerging levels of English language development. This includes ELs who are coming into schools from countries and commonwealths outside of the United States and have no prior experience with English and those learners born in the United States who are entering school for the first time. For the purposes of this book, ELs who are from literacy-oriented families and who have attended school for a commensurate amount of time as their U.S. peers in their home countries are considered beginners *at least* through the first year of school. Those students who do not routinely practice literacy behaviors and have little or no former schooling may be at the beginning stage of English acquisition for a longer period of time.

With all of these dynamics and changes that are occurring in the nation, schools that were once predominantly populated with monolingual English-fluent students are now finding themselves working with an emerging or continuously growing population of ELs. While this population of students is increasing quickly, their overall progress is very poor. The number of ELs who speak English and fail to complete high school is three times that of the general population, and ELs who struggle to use English—a significant and growing number—fail at five times the rate of the general population (August & Shanahan, 2006). Most are performing half as well as their native-English-speaking peers, many are failing, and a significant number drop out of school. Equally troubling is the fact that of those who complete high school successfully and are admitted to college, the vast majority quit (August & Shanahan, 2006; Goldenberg & Coleman, 2010).

While many educational scholars, policy experts, and practitioners have identified various reasons for these outcomes, little has recently been written about how to address students who are at the beginning stages of learning English. We believe that it is paramount to support educators to be proactive in addressing the needs of beginning-level ELs. The example that we provided in the start of this chapter is illustrative of some schools that have not taken the time needed to think through what should be in place for ELs and their families. Indeed, we know that many schools are making efforts to be more welcoming and inviting, and it is not our intent to be dismissive or to paint the nation's schools with a broad brush. However, the absence of paying intentional focus to the growing population of beginning ELs and their families contributes heavily to the failures that are occurring. Further, while we believe that bilingualism is important and many schools are including bilingual support in various forms, the presence of the native language alone does not set the stage for success. Rather, schools must consider the ways in which new English speakers and their families are

- welcomed into the classroom and school community,
- honored as learners, and
- considered assets.

We call this reflecting on the *Big Picture* of what we know as school.

RESOURCES FOR LEADERS AND TEACHERS OF BEGINNING LEARNERS OF ENGLISH

While much has been written about the general population of ELs (including by us), very little of what has recently been written has focused on starting or beginning-level learners of English. Let's go to another typical scenario when a new EL enters school in the United States: When Eduardo's family brought him to the kindergarten screening meeting at his new school, a team of educators that included his classroom teacher, an administrator, and a speech and language pathologist greeted them. The school regularly schedules this type of meeting to learn about each new student entering kindergarten. Before meeting with Eduardo and his parents, the team learned that he had been born in the same city that their school was located in, had not attended preschool, and had been cared for by his grandparents while his parents worked. When Eduardo and his family arrived, his teacher greeted them in English. While his father was able to answer some questions in English, most of the questions were answered with polite nods. Similarly, Eduardo was not able to answer any substantive questions. While his classroom teacher knew some greeting words in Spanish, she and the team could not interact in Spanish and were not able to learn much about Eduardo. After the meeting, they looked at each other and almost simultaneously asked the other, "How is it possible that a child born in the United States does not speak English? Let's give him the placement test to see how much English he has and decide what to do." Their plan is not unusual. Indeed, it is customary in almost all public schools across our nation. Information about proficiency levels in English is, by far, the most common means for determining the needs of students who are learning

English. While it is very helpful information, it is not comprehensive. What is missing, as we detail in this book, places ELs at a significant disadvantage. There is an urgent need for a more appropriate means to address the needs of beginning-level EL.

While over half of our nation's beginning ELs are born in the United States and the remainder have just arrived from other countries, all of these learners are at a distinct disadvantage compared to their native-English-speaking peers. That is, they rely on their educators and schools to help them gain equal access to the learning environment. Although the right to gain access is required under federal Office of Civil Rights (OCR) (2005) regulations, the means that schools use for students to gain this important access is often marginal.

CHALLENGES FACED BY BEGINNING ENGLISH LEARNERS AND THEIR FAMILIES

Students at the first stages of learning English are generally not familiar with American school culture, American public schools, or being learners in these settings. While this is particularly true for students born in countries other than the United States, even if beginning ELs are born in the this country, they are likely not familiar with the dominant culture—that being monolingual English—and are more than likely being taught by a dominant population of white middle-class monolingual-English-speaking educators who are not accustomed to working with linguistic-minority learners (Hollins & Guzman, 2005; Ladson-Billings, 1995).

All ELs at the beginning stages are not familiar with English and cannot use it to learn. In addition, many of the students who are new to the United States have come from countries whose educational system is significantly different than that of the United States. For example, some ELs did not attend school on a regular basis, others attended for a few hours a week, and still others come from countries where children begin school at a later age than in the United States. We discuss these differences in more detail in Chapter 2.

WHAT IS BEING DONE TO ADDRESS THE NEEDS OF BEGINNING ENGLISH LEARNERS?

In an effort to address these gaps and challenges, many districts are scrambling to find the right answers to help their ELs succeed. Because this is a fast-growing population, some schools are being reactive to the growth as opposed to being proactive about it. Rather than create programming and plans for the certainty that beginning speakers of English will enroll, schools use a "wait and see" approach, figuring that the best means for educating ELs is to do so as it is happening. In the scenario at the opening of this chapter, for example, the school secretary responds with "We'll have to figure something out."

Some schools isolate ELs from English-speaking peers (Gándara, 2010). Perhaps their thinking is that students who are not yet familiar with the language need a completely separate program. Indeed, among the nation's schools, beginning-level ELs are often separated from their English-speaking peers by virtue of being placed in classrooms in which they do not associate with native English speakers and/or are isolated by being taken out of the classroom (Gándara, 2010). Other schools believe that ELs should be part of the whole school and provide them with an educational program that is almost entirely in the general classroom, figuring that these students learn best by being immersed with fluent English speakers (Haynes, 2007b; Zacarian, 2011). This response is made with the assumption that students learn English best on their own through an immersion experience and does not pay particular attention to the language, cultural, and learning needs of ELs. As a result, most are finding that these approaches are not successful.

To address these gaps and challenges, some schools are drawing from various models of English language and academic development (which we discuss in Chapter 4), including bilingual education, sheltered instruction, structured immersion, and English as a second language, assuming that these will address all of their ELs' needs. Others are purchasing textbook series that have accompanying supplemental materials for ELs. In these instances, schools hope that these modifications will satisfy what is needed to help them effectively address the needs of their ELs as they enroll in school.

Unfortunately, these programs and textbooks have not shown the positive growth for beginning ELs that is sorely needed. The OCR, a division of the U.S. Department of Education, has been investigating programs for ELs across our nation (Frankenberg, Siegel-Hawley, & Wang, 2010, p. 4). It is doing this in light of the poor outcomes of this population of students, their isolation in public schools, and poor communications with EL parents. In fact, U.S. educational officials have designated equal access to quality education as the civil rights issue of our generation (US Department of Education, October 6, 2011). The education of ELs plays a significant part in this designation. In addition, the advent of public charter schools has prompted further investigation by the OCR as recent reports on charter schools have found that they "stratify students by race, class and possibly language . . . [and] are more racially isolated than traditional public schools in virtually every state and large metropolitan area in the nation" (Frankenberg et al., 2010, p. 4).

The situations described in the scenarios in this chapter are emblematic of many schools. Whether they have large or small populations of ELs, educators have not yet figured out how to welcome this growing population into the fold of what we call school. They do not have procedures in place to meet the needs of beginning-level ELs.

Whereas much has been written about teaching ELs, including books that we have written on this topic, little has been written for these specific stages of English language acquisition as a whole school–whole community effort. There is an urgent need for this way of thinking.

Perhaps the political climate for educating ELs has perpetuated our lack of responsiveness for students who are just beginning to learn English or the lack of available resources for beginning speakers of English and the preparation of their teachers. Regardless of the reasons, beginning ELs are all too often an isolated and marginalized population in U.S. schools and, at the same time, the most vulnerable and at-risk-of-failing population.

When students and their families do not feel welcomed into the community, such as in Mei's case, it can foretell a troublesome future. When a student is not valued and honored as a learner and member of the school, and parents are equally disconnected from the important introductory process, their investment in learning and being connected as members can range from being significantly impacted to destroyed. The importance of the transition process from one language and culture to another cannot be minimized. This involves the need to learn a new language, the explicit and implicit rules of a new culture (including that of the school), and the academic content and thinking skills needed to learn in the context of a U.S. public school.

USING A THREE-PHASE PLANNING APPROACH FOR BEGINNING LEARNERS OF ENGLISH

Much has been written about the merits of early intervention. Early intervention programs are those in which students' needs are addressed when they enroll in school and, when appropriate, before school begins. The rationale for this thinking is that students will receive much-needed support as it is needed and to the degree in which it is needed so that they may be ready to learn grade-level content and be active members of their learning communities. Such well-known educational activities as preschool programming and *Response to Intervention,* in which schools systematically provide interventions when they are needed to prevent students from failing (Hamayan, Marler, Sanchez-Lopez, & Damico, 2007), speak to the advantages of our being proactive about using early intervention techniques. Similarly, schools need specific, well-developed and proven-to-be-effective programming that addresses the sociocultural, language, academic, and thinking skill needs of beginning ELs.

Also, parents of ELs must be welcomed into their child's school. When parents and students do not speak English, the barrier for them to access school and for the school to access them can seem and be overwhelming. Addressing the needs of entry and beginning ELs and their families requires that we think intentionally and anew about the ways in which our schools are prepared for this growing population as they enroll in our schools. In this book, we provide a means for schools to be intentionally responsive to the needs of entry- and beginning-level ELs and their families.

In this book, we present a three-pronged approach for creating an environment in which ELs and their families are intentionally prepared to be active participants and members of their school communities as they enroll in a school for a first exposure to English. This approach consists of the following steps:

1. Identify and implement what is needed for beginning ELs and their families to be assets and active members of the classroom and school communities in a social and academic way.

2. Design and modify instructional programming for entry- and beginning-level learners of English.

3. Provide professional development to all school personnel so that the school environment and academic programs are inclusive of beginning-level ELs.

SUMMARY

In this chapter, we described the increasing number of ELs in the nation's public and public charter schools, highlighting the following:

- the growth of ELs in relation to the total general student population
- the number of languages represented
- the academic performance outcomes of ELs
- what we mean by "beginning ELs"
- our rationale for using a three-pronged approach to create an environment in which ELs and their families are active participants and members of their school community

2 Taking a Closer Look

Angel and his mother moved from a small agrarian community in Mexico to a town in Mississippi where they were reunited with his father, who had been in the United States working as a landscaper for a local garden center. When Angel's parents enrolled him in school, he was given a language test that determined that he was a beginning-level English learner (EL). With this information, he was placed in an English as a second language (ESL) class for 40 minutes a day to learn English. Angel spent the rest of the day in an English-only environment where he was expected to learn math, science, social studies, and other academic subjects. In his ESL class, some of his peers were beginning-level ELs like Angel, while others were nearly proficient in English.

Most of Angel's peers came from homes in which parents were affiliated with a local university as graduate students or in professional positions. Angel was often lost in his classes, including his ESL class. He spent most of his time trying feverishly to mimic what he thought his peers were doing. He also found it impossible to make friends for two reasons: He didn't speak English, and his Latino peers did not want to befriend someone from a dramatically lower socioeconomic status. During the end-of-year parent conference, his classroom and ESL teachers recommended that he repeat the third grade, stating that he had not made sufficient progress in English to be promoted. The school believed that they had made the right decision and concurred, after his parents left the meeting, that Angel was probably "another student with a learning disability." His classroom teacher even professed to thinking that he had a low level of intelligence.

To understand more about Angel and students like him, it's helpful to discuss the continuum of literacy orientations among the students who are entering our classrooms (Haynes & Zacarian, 2010; Pransky, 2009; Zacarian, 2011). By taking a closer look at how literacy development affects the learning of the students in U.S. classrooms, we can develop a more comprehensive understanding about our students and a more effective instructional approach for them.

INFLUENCE OF LITERACY

Marina is a student in Angel's ESL class, and her parents are graduate students at the university. Marina routinely observes her parents reading a cookbook or a newspaper, or studying. When Marina's parents speak to her, they use a high level of Russian vocabulary and complex sentence structures. Also, they frequently interact with her using a lot of spoken Russian. She has observed these behaviors since birth and began engaging in them at a young age. Parents like Marina's practice important literacy behaviors such as helping their children use higher order thinking skills at young ages and encouraging them to move toward independent thinking. For example, at an outing at a local children's museum to see an exhibit on dinosaurs, Marina's father asked her, "Why do you think the Tyrannosaurus rex has sharp teeth?" Higher order questions such as this are commonplace in literacy-oriented homes and represent a clear developmental focus on helping children develop adult-like thinking and problem-solving skills at young ages.

According to Pransky (2008, 2009) the parenting practices commonly associated with these behaviors reflect parents' placing importance on observing children's behavior and providing coaching as needed. To understand more about these practices and behaviors, it is important to consider the cultural context in which they occur (Rogoff, 1990). Being oriented to school requires that children be reared in communities where language behaviors, customs, and structures are implicitly and explicitly focused on formal education. It also requires that children engage actively in these behaviors as part of their development. For example, Marina's parents and the social groups in which she is raised provide her with multiple experiences that she can, in turn, bring to her own literacy development. Some of these include playing computer games that are targeted to enhance the development of her listening, speaking, reading, and writing skills. Indeed, many families raise computer-literate children who come to school with knowledge of technology and are familiar with using computers for educational purposes (Pransky, 2009). Marina came to the United States equipped with this knowledge.

DIFFERENCES IN LITERACY AND EDUCATIONAL EXPERIENCES

A significant and growing number of ELs in the U.S. are being reared in families that are not formally educated or have limited prior educational experiences (Pransky, 2008; August & Shanahan, 2006). Because literacy development begins at a young age, it is greatly influenced by a child's home and context (Lesaux & Geva, 2006; Rogoff, 1990). The distinctions between students that are rigorously exposed to school-matched literacy behaviors from birth and those that have not had this routine intentional exposure or degree of it is important to understand. It has deep meaning in terms of what must be considered to create an optimal learning environment for all English learners.

Rogoff (1990) provides us with a lens to understand some of the distinctions between what Pransky (2009) calls *literacy-oriented* and *non-literacy-oriented* ELs. Literacy-oriented ELs have been reared in communities that are focused on helping children develop the organizational, categorizing, cause-and-effect, and other cognitive skills that match what will occur in school. At the other end of the literacy continuum, ELs are also engaged in apprenticeships, but these are more experientially and contextually based. Think of Angel's father's farming background. For Angel to become a good gardener, he would typically watch his father completing the important tasks of growing produce and learning how to master the needed tasks explicitly. Indeed, parenting is not as geared for the development of adult-like thinking or problem-solving skills in children. Students from these experiences and communities are expected to develop these skills when they are adults (Pransky, 2009).

DIFFERENCES IN ORIENTATION TO TIME

Time is one of the most central differences that separate cultures and cultural ways of doing things. Dominant U.S. culture is time-centric (Hall, 1983; Haynes & Zacarian, 2010). There is a common reverence for efficiency. The common mantra "time is money" is a way to describe this type of thinking. Time is valued economically, personally, and professionally. It represents a monochromic approach to time and favors a linear focus on timeliness (Hall, 1990). That is, a cultural way of being and thinking is focused on the time of day, day of the week, week in the month, month in the year, and so forth. If we look back at Marina, we see that she comes from a monochromic culture in Russia. Her parents' value behaviors such as arriving at school on time as well as regular school attendance and reflect American monochromic orientation toward time. Indeed, they carve out time every day for Marina to do homework and for them to provide help as needed. They are familiar with the cultural meaning of "getting things done on time" because they know that time is highly valued.

Many beginning ELs do not come from a monochromic culture. They come from relationship-oriented polychromic cultures. Feelings and emotions are foremost, and objective facts are of secondary importance (Hall, 1983). Further, the flow of information communicated from parent/guardian to child has immediate relevance; learning that is necessary at some future date is not considered important (DeCapua & Marshall, 2011). Indeed, time passes on an unlimited continuum. Things get done in their own time. Because of this, people from monochromic cultures often perceive people from polychromic cultures as being late. For people from a polychromic culture, exact times and schedules are not important. Angel is often very late for school, and he continually misses school for family reasons. Family relationships take precedence in polychromic cultures. Angel's parents lack cultural understanding of "school schedules" and the necessity of coming at the assigned time.

Fundamentally, we have found that beginning ELs and their families' represent a polychromic culture and a significant number are not exposed to literacy as a cultural way of being and acting. Classrooms must be in a position of providing for such learners. However, the differences among literacy and backgrounds, as well as monochromic and polychromic groups, are important to discuss. Why? As educators, we engage in a high level of literacy-oriented and monochromic behaviors and beliefs that represent this group and not the other. Drawing from Pransky's terminology of "literacy and non-literacy orientation" (2009), Figure 2.1 highlights the commonalities and differences between beginning ELs from literacy and non-literacy orientations.

THREE DIFFERENT TYPES OF STUDENTS

ELs with less formal educational and literacy experiences manifest themselves in various ways. One particular challenge in U.S. schools is a student with limited or interrupted prior formal education, commonly referred to as SLIFE. Drawing from DeCapua and Marshall (2011), we describe these students in three ways:

1. They may come from countries where schooling is not mandated; therefore, they have no knowledge of school. For example, they

Figure 2.1 Differences and Commonalities Between Literacy- and Non-Literacy-Oriented Beginning ELs

Literacy Oriented	Commonalities	Non-Literacy Oriented
Parents have a formal education. Literacy oriented behaviors can be observed at home. Time is highly valued. Students engage in developing formal literacy skills at a young age, including higher order and independent thinking skills. Learning is relevant in the future. Children's learning is academic. Home practices are closely related to school practices.	The primary language is one other than English. Students are at the beginning proficiency stages of learning English.	Parents are not formally educated. Oral traditions are important in transferring knowledge at home. Relationships are highly valued. Students do not engage in literacy practices at home. They learn from following parents' model and completing pragmatic tasks. Learning is immediately relevant. Children's learning is contextualized by parents. Experiences at home are not directed to school-matched behaviors.

may not know how to hold a pencil or sit on a chair. There may not be a written language, or written language is a relatively new development.

2. They may begin school in one place and continually move, as is the case for many children of migrant workers. In this case, prolonged absences and changes in schools are commonplace. ELs may also come to the United States but travel frequently back to their home countries for extended amounts of time.

3. They may have attended school regularly in their native countries, but the quality of that education was significantly less than that of a U.S. education and they are several years behind their U.S. peers. This lack of quality education may be due to inadequate resources, a shortage of trained teachers, parents' lack of funds to pay for school, frequently occurring weather conditions that interrupt schooling (as is the case for some Indian students whose schools close during the rainy season), or the type of schooling they received.

STUDENTS EXPERIENCING TRAUMA

Layered on the top of the complexities of working with students with varied literacy backgrounds are students who have experienced significant trauma in their lives. This could be due to war, natural disaster, dramatic poverty, or other major impacting stressors. Students who have these experiences represent all levels of the literacy spectrum. However, the traumatic disruption that they have experienced is significantly distinct from what would have been typical to their development. Behaviors ranging from impulsivity to hypervigilance are not unusual because students have lived or are living in a tumultuous setting and respond to trauma in a range of ways (Craig, 2008). A child who experienced the tsunami in Japan and lost his parents and other family members may be more likely to come from a literacy-oriented home than would children who experienced the earthquake in Haiti. Children from these two disaster areas who enter the United States will have educational needs that are quite different even though they share the horrific disruptive experience of a natural disaster.

ELs from traumatic backgrounds may also come from a variety of African countries where genocide interrupted their schooling for many years—if it was available at all. Trauma is an integral part of their lives and deeply affects their capacity to learn and develop socially and emotionally in the way that students do when they have not experienced these disruptions. Because trauma is so relevant, we devote Chapter 8 to this important topic.

Figure 2.2 illustrates the overlap of trauma of the diverse population of ELs.

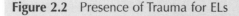

Figure 2.2   Presence of Trauma for ELs

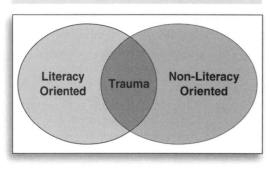

HOW POVERTY AFFECTS LEARNING

An important distinction among ELs in relation to the total population of American public school students is that so many live in poverty. Indeed, almost 70% of all ELs in the United States live 200% below the poverty level ("A Distinct Population," 2009; Goldenberg & Coleman, 2010). Unlike peers whose families have more economic opportunities, ELs are among the poorest in our nation's schools.

According to educational researcher Diane Ravitch (2011), there is already an achievement gap when children enter kindergarten. Students who live in poverty have diminished chances of succeeding in school. While there is a correlation between the level of poverty and literacy and numeracy (Denny, 2002), we have to consider what this means in context. In the case of students living in poverty and in contexts where literacy behaviors are not practiced, exposure to literacy and numeracy practices are more dependent on what occurs in school than in the case of peers who come from homes in which literacy behaviors are practiced. However, as we discuss this book, we view all students as having many rich assets that can and should be honored and valued by their teachers. This can only occur when teachers have a deep understanding of their students and draw from their students' resources in the planning and delivery of instruction. To discuss this further requires that we look more closely at the language we have used to describe ELs from different literacy experiences.

Gonzalez, Moll, and Amanti (2005) describe all people as having important *funds of knowledge*. In this book, we offer many examples of how teachers can create an asset-based model that draws from these funds. An asset-based ideology of teaching occurs when instruction is deeply connected to our students, their families and their communities.

While all ELs need cultural sensitivity and effective and well-developed programming to learn English and academic matters, students from families with limited formal education and literacy must be provided with programming that pays focused and intentional attention to literacy behavior development so that ELs from this group may develop these critical practices.

INDIVIDUALISTIC AND COLLECTIVIST CULTURES

Another difference among ELs entering our schools is that some are from individualistic cultures and others collectivistic cultures. In the former, individual rights supersede duty to one's family, clan, ethnic group, or nation. In general, members of the dominant U.S. culture believe that children should be raised to think and judge independently. The goal of education is to have children learn to think like adults when they are still children. Children's efforts to think and use their independent thinking skills are praised and rewarded. Their wants, needs, and desires are often viewed as of primary concern in the family.

Many ELs come from collectivistic cultures in which the good of the individual is sacrificed to the good of the group. A person's moral worth is judged by how much he or she sacrifices himself to the group. Students from this type of culture work best when they can form a relationship with the group. They are *we* rather than *I* oriented. These factors are urgently important for all teachers and administrators to know.

ADDRESSING THE COMPLEX NEEDS OF ENGLISH LEARNERS

Fundamentally, how ELs are welcomed into our schools and the instruction they receive greatly determine their success in school. As educators, we have to be powerfully dedicated to understanding the backgrounds of our diverse populations of ELs, including those (1) who are academic language learners and do not yet possess the literacy skills that they need to succeed in school, (2) who are from polychromic cultures, (3) who have experienced trauma and violence, and/or (4) who are living in poverty.

Schools in the United States are basically developed around the idea that students will be from literacy-based cultures. As a group, teachers in the United States are predominately white, middle class, and female (Honawar, 2009; Ladson-Billings, 1995; Zeichner & Hoeft, 1996). We know what to do with students who come from this background. However, there is a mismatch between the linguistically and culturally diverse students who are actually sitting in classrooms and the teachers who teach them. This mismatch may occur even if schools hire teachers who come from diverse backgrounds but who come from literacy-oriented homes.

One of the primary problems for children with these diverse experiences is that their programming is often not tailored to their needs (Zacarian, 2011). As opposed to carefully considering the significant needs of students from these diverse backgrounds, English proficiency is the only factor that is considered. Beginning-level learners pose a particular problem because many perceive that their primary need is to be able to converse socially in English and that, once this occurs, learning in an academic setting will follow.

For schools to create an optimal learning environment for beginning-level ELs, we believe that certain fundamental elements must be included.

The first is that schools must identify who their ELs are according to the information we have provided in this chapter:

1. Is the student U.S. born or from a country or commonwealth outside of the continental United States?

2. What is the literacy orientation of the student's family?

3. What is the student's educational history? What kind of school did the student have in his or her home country?

4. Has the student experienced trauma? If so, what type?

5. What is the socioeconomic status of the child's family?

6. Are they from a monochromic or polychromic culture?

7. Are they from an individualistic or collectivist culture?

Regardless of a child's prior literacy or life experiences (traumatic or not), socioeconomic status, and/or beliefs about individualism or collectivism, schools must provide an appropriate intake procedure and develop an asset-based model of programming.

Knowing that most educators are white, middle class, and possessing little experience with or training in teaching beginning ELs (Ladson-Billings, 1995; Zeichner & Hoeft, 1996), we approach this issue with the belief that we can provide programming that fits the needs of this dynamically growing population with specific strategies that will support the success of all students. Chapter 3 focuses on this element of the entry-level program for ELs.

SUMMARY

In this chapter, we began to explore the diverse population of ELs in order to provide a more comprehensive picture of their needs. While all ELs require educators to be sensitive to their English learning needs, it is critically important to understand the complex differences among this population to plan programming that is effective. In this chapter we explained the distinctions pertaining to the following:

- ELs being reared in communities where language, behaviors, customs, and structures are implicitly and explicitly focused on formal education

- ELs being reared in communities where language, customs, and structures are not focused on or exposed to formal education behaviors
- ELs from monochromic versus polychromic cultures
- ELs experiencing trauma and violence
- ELs living in poverty

Drawing from this chapter and Chapter 1, the next chapter focuses on key elements to consider in identifying ELs and creating effective programming that takes into account the diverse needs of this population.

3 Effective Programming for English Learners

Central Valley School District is located in an old industrial city in the northeastern United States. Its population of English learners (ELs) has grown from 75 to 300 in the short span of 3 years. Unfortunately, many are performing poorly on state assessments, despite the various initiatives that are occurring, and the superintendent has called a meeting with the district's principals to discuss this outcome. Mrs. Reid is the principal of the high school. Half of the ELs in her school failed the 10th-grade English and mathematics exams. Mr. Lombardini is one of the middle school principals. To prepare for the meeting, he reviewed the performance of ELs on the state's most recent assessment of eighth-grade English language arts and mathematics and noted that the majority did not meet the state benchmark. Mr. Kelly is a new elementary school principal in the district. As he gathers information for the meeting about the ELs in the district's elementary schools, he learns that the programming for elementary ELs has been in existence for over 20 years. Thinking that this means the school has clear routines and practices, he hopes that he can strengthen whatever is needed.

As the Central Valley administrators begin to look at the programming for ELs in their schools, they find that there is strong commitment among the leadership team but a lack of consistency. A primary example is the disparate amount of time that ELs receive instruction in English as a second language (ESL) classes. At the elementary level, beginning ELs receive 30 minutes each day, whereas at the middle and high schools they receive 2 hours. The administrators also discover that only one high school parent of an EL participates on the school district's parent advisory committee. They also identify several prevailing district attitudes and practices, as laid out in Box 3.1.

> ### BOX 3.1   Prevailing Attitudes and Practices in the Central Valley School District
>
> - There is no systematic routine for gaining enrollment information from families other than by performing the state-required identification assessment.
> - ESL is considered a remedial rather than developmental program, and at the high school, credit is not given for ESL classes.
> - One of the elementary schools offers bilingual education programming, but the others do not.
> - Students who enroll during the school year (and many beginners do) are placed with the teachers who have the least number of students, and many of these teachers have not had any professional development on working with ELs.
> - In the elementary and middle schools, the master school schedule is driven by special education and/or specials such as art and music.
> - While it is not intended, in practice, ELs are randomly pulled out of math, science, and social studies classes to attend ESL or go without any ESL or support in their primary language.

As the meeting continues, each administrator becomes more and more aware of how inconsistent their programming is for ELs. The district superintendent charges some of the elementary, middle, and high school principals to co-lead an effort to create systemic districtwide policies and procedures for ELs. Mr. Lombardini, Mrs. Reid, and Mr. Kelly volunteer for this work. One of their goals is to gather as broad a representation as possible to collaboratively engage in this work. They assemble a team of ESL, grade-level, and secondary subject matter teachers, guidance staff, parents, and community members to meet with them. They believe that a team effort will help raise the level of their ELs' academic performance.

DEVELOPING A DISTRICTWIDE EFFORT

The efforts of the Central Valley School District exemplify what is possible when districts engage in a collaborative effort to build a community of learners in which all students, including ELs, are considered an essential part of the whole (Zacarian, 2011). Why? ELs are a frequently marginalized group that is often not factored into the learning and whole-school environment (Cummins, 2001, Zacarian, 2007). Further, it is not uncommon for ESL and/or bilingual classes to be on one side of a building or in small group rooms or spaces away from the mainstream. Also, ELs' course schedules and school day can be fragmented as a result of trying to "add" English language development or ESL and bilingual classes or classes with bilingual support as opposed to making them part of the core curriculum and offerings. Further, programming for ELs, as in Central Valley, may differ from grade to grade within a school, from school to school, and from district to district (Zacarian, 2007, 2011). In addition, while a school may declare that it offers bilingual education, sheltered instruction, or other program types, model names such as these mean a myriad of differing things in practice (Soltero, 2004; Zacarian, 2011). Programming is discussed further in Chapter 4.

For example, at Mrs. Reid's high school, the term *bilingual programming* means that paraprofessionals work in content classrooms translating instruction into a student's native language. In Mr. Lombardini's middle school, it means that a bilingual teacher provides instruction. In Mr. Kelly's elementary school, it refers to the support that is given to beginning-level ELs from third through fifth grade—while none is given to ELs in kindergarten through second grade. In addition, some students in Mr. Kelly's school are given extra time for ESL instruction, whereas others are not. In practice, kindergarten and first-grade ELs receive 30 minutes of ESL a day, whereas fifth-grade ELs receive an hour. Think of the inconsistencies in this district.

One reason for these outcomes is that ELs and their schedules are often considered after the fact as opposed to as an integral part of the whole-school curriculum, course of study, and environment (Soltero, 2004; Zacarian, 2011). The three building principals discuss their concerns about these inconsistencies. As they talk, they realize that each has witnessed some of their ELs being taken out of classes, such as science and social studies, to attend ESL classes. Mrs. Reid has also seen parents waiting for assistance for too long in the front and guidance offices. Mr. Lombardini has observed that ELs are often moving through the hallways to attend ESL classes while most of their peers' classes are in session.

As Mrs. Reid, Mr. Kelly, and Mr. Lombardini organize the group's first meeting, they are not sure where to begin. So much seems to be going wrong. How can they make it right? They wisely decide that it is prudent to begin by addressing the needs of the newest students, the ones who are coming to their schools as beginning learners of English. They will then build programming from the beginning-level EL to the EL who demonstrates proficiency in English. To address the former, they create a series of questions that will be asked at the first meeting:

1. What is our enrollment process for ELs?

2. How do we identify ELs and inform their parents about our findings?

3. How are ELs scheduled for classes?

4. What model are we using to deliver instruction?

5. How will we use this data to inform our decisions?

REVIEWING THE ENROLLMENT PROCESS

A review of a school's enrollment process is an essential first step. To understand why this is so important, let's look at the first meeting that the three principals hold with the team. The first issue that they consider is the enrollment process for ELs. They examine copies of the schools' enrollment forms, which include the home language survey, the daily schedule, the school calendar, course information, immunization forms, the emergency information form, copies of student's rights, and the code of conduct. The three principals wonder whether all of the documents have been translated, how long they took to complete, and whether a staff member covers the information in the packet with parents and their children.

The group realizes how important it is to note that not everyone knows the answers to these questions. As a remedy, they discuss the following question: How do we make the enrollment process welcoming and transparent for parents and our school personnel and, at the same time, obtain all of the information that is needed to enroll students appropriately?

IDENTIFYING ENGLISH LEARNERS

Federal regulations, as described by the U.S. Department of Education, Office of Civil Rights (1991), requires schools to have procedures in place for identifying ELs, to complete these procedures within a specific time span, and to notify parents of the assessment results. Under federal law, specifically Subsection 3202 of U.S. Department of Education's Elementary and Secondary Regulations, parents must be notified within 30 days of the beginning of the school year and within 2 weeks during any other time during the school year.

Schools are also required to provide parents with information about their child's level of English proficiency and how this was determined, the type of program that their child is enrolled in or recommended to participate in, and the method of instruction that is used to support the learning of English and academic content. State education agencies commonly provide public and public charter schools with a list of specific tests that must be administered for this identification purpose. A project recently completed by Colorín Colorado (Zacarian, 2012) provides information about

each state's identification requirements. These may be found at www
.colorincolorado.org/web_resources/by_state.

In addition, it is very helpful, when possible, to assess students in English
and their primary language. This greatly helps in understanding a student's language and literacy development and is a critical element for
bilingual programming when it is implemented. It is important to note,
however, that some states prohibit bilingual programming, and it is
important to check individual state education agencies' regulations to
determine what is acceptable. In situations where bilingual assessments
can be employed, the Student Oral Language Observation Matrix (SOLOM),
created by the California Department of Education, provides a means to
assess students' ability to listen and speak in any language (Lindholm-
Leary, 2001). It is helpful for assessing the primary languages of students
who speak languages other than English and Spanish (see Resource 3.1 for
a sample of the SOLOM).

It is also important for school communities to know and be familiar
with the federal definition of an EL. The official federal definition, referred
to as a student who is *limited English proficient* (U.S. Department of Education, 2004), is presented in Box 3.2.

BOX 3.2   Federal Definition of English Learner

(25) The term limited English proficient, when used with respect to an individual,
means an individual—

  (A) who is aged 3 through 21;

  (B) who is enrolled or preparing to enroll in an elementary school or second-
       ary school;

  (C) (i)   who was not born in the United States or whose native language is
             a language other than English;

       (ii) (I)   who is a Native American or Alaska Native, or a native resident
                   of the outlying areas; and

             (II) who comes from an environment where a language other than
                   English has had a significant impact on the individual's level of
                   English language proficiency; or

       (iii) who is migratory, whose native language is a language other than
             English, and who comes from an environment where a language
             other than English is dominant; and

(Continued)

(Continued)

(D) whose difficulties in speaking, reading, writing, or understanding the English language may be sufficient to deny the individual—

    (i) the ability to meet the State's proficient level of achievement on State assessments described in section 1111(b)(3);

    (ii) the ability to successfully achieve in classrooms where the language of instruction is English; or

    (iii) the opportunity to participate fully in society.

Source: U.S. Department of Education (2004).

In general terms (Zacarian, 2012) an EL is a student who is in the process of acquiring English and has a first language other than or in addition to English. In addition, the laws do not place restrictions on the amount of time that is needed for an English learner to

- be able to listen, speak, read, and write in English;
- be successful in classroom settings where English is the language of instruction;
- be able to participate actively in their classroom, school, community, and beyond.

Typically, enrollment must be a two-way process in which parents and schools furnish each other with information. This generally occurs before the identification process begins. Figure 3.1 provides a list of the enrollment activities.

In the United States, the Food and Drug Administration requires, with some exemptions, that all school-age public and public charter school children have updated immunizations. It is common for parents to bring documents signed by their child's doctor or public health or other department attesting that their child has been immunized. While this is a routine practice, it may not be familiar to newly immigrated families and can forestall the enrollment of their children. The same is true for prior school transcripts and birth certificates. Some parents know that these documents are needed, but others might not. In addition, some refugees, immigrant parents, and others may not have transcripts, or these documents may be written in a language other than English, making the process of translating and understanding the content challenging for schools. Thus, key required documents pose distinct challenges for parents and schools alike. This issue is further compounded by the fact that many students from countries

Figure 3.1   Enrollment Process

Step 1. Parents generally bring

- Immunization forms
- Child's prior school transcripts
- Birth certificate
- Proof of residency

Step 2. Parents generally complete

- Home language survey
- Emergency information
- Free and reduced lunch application process
- Prior transcript release form

Step 3. Parents typically must understand Steps 1 and 2 as well as

- Prior transcript review process
- Daily schedule, school calendar
- Course information
- Immunization process
- Emergency process
- Student's rights and code of conduct
- Extracurricular activities
- Identification and program placement process for ELs

that have been torn apart by war or natural disasters will not have a birth certificate and may have to use a passport or documents supplied by their embassy.

In addition, parents must complete several enrollment forms. These generally include a home language survey, an emergency information card, and a form granting permission to release prior transcripts if these have not been furnished. Many parents are not familiar with the purpose of these forms and might be completing them without understanding what they mean. One staff member recalled a time when the school activated the emergency card information to phone parents that school was being released early due to a snowstorm. The call confused many of the parents of ELs who did not speak English.

HELPING PARENTS UNDERSTAND THE ENROLLMENT PROCESS

It is important for parents and their child's school to understand the rationale for the forms that must be completed. For example, let's look at the purpose of the home language survey (see Resource 3.2). Its intent is to support the school in determining which students should be assessed in order to identify the ELs in a school and district so that these students can be provided with appropriate programming. Parents may not understand its purpose or may even be afraid that if they write a language other than English their child might be denied an education.

The same holds true for each of the forms that parents must complete. Without knowing the purpose of each form, parents may, understandably, make misassumptions about them and schools may not gather accurate information. For example, if parents do not understand the purpose of the emergency information card, they may change their phone number without notifying the school or give the number of a neighbor or friend who does not know that he or she has been listed as an emergency contact.

Potential ELs should be assessed for English language development services as soon as possible. While the federal guidelines, as quoted earlier, provide a timeline for this purpose, state education agencies should be consulted to determine the span that is allowed, as some require a quicker process—and for good reason. It is essential that students be identified as quickly as possible to determine the type of programming that is needed. A good plan is to identify ELs within the first 5 days of enrollment. In Mr. Kelly's school, for example, students were assigned to classrooms before the EL identification process had occurred. This created a good number of difficulties, the most prominent being determining the number of teachers needed to teach ESL, provide bilingual instruction, and, of course, schedule classes. Collaboratively, the team at Central Valley adopted a policy whereby students whose parents indicated on the home language survey that a language other than or in addition to English is used would be given identification testing the week before school began. Any student who enrolled during the school year would be tested within 5 days of enrollment. Further, parents would be notified within 5 days after the testing was administered.

Central Valley implemented a form to document the test findings (see Resource 3.3). The intent of the form is to provide each student's teacher with information about the student's language assessment findings. The second page of the form includes a short description of each proficiency level; the intent of this section is to help teachers match their instruction with the student's proficiency level.

The assessments and tools that the team created also include a parent/student interview for identified ELs (see Resource 3.4). The interview would be conducted by guidance and bilingual staff who would gather information about the student's prior schooling, language of instruction, and background experiences to further support the building of an appropriate educational program. They believed that the information that they would be gathering would greatly help them create and implement more successful programming.

Once the Central Valley School District introduced procedures for identifying ELs, the committee asked themselves what their next steps should be. What should they do with this information to help them build effective and comprehensive programming for beginning learners of English and other ELs? How can they improve the learning environment for ELs?

As a start, they decided to analyze the data that they gathered from identifying the district's ELs, as they knew that it was critical for them to understand their EL population in order to build programming for them. For example, while they knew that many of the district's students spoke Spanish and Haitian Creole, they did not know such important data as the grade levels, prior literacy experiences, and English proficiency levels of the district's ELs. They created a separate category for all of the information that they believed they needed. This included the languages the ELs speak, the countries that they come from, their English language development levels, students who have had interrupted schooling, students who receive free or reduced lunch, and ELs who receive Title 1 services. This information is greatly helpful for schools to use in determining the appropriateness of various program model options. With this information in hand, along with the changes that were made in the enrollment process, the Central Valley EL committee believed that their programming would be stronger and that their students would benefit from their collaborative efforts.

SUMMARY

In this chapter, we focused on the key elements that should be included in identifying English learners. The chapter highlighted the following:

- the federal laws regarding the identification of ELs
- the importance and process of gathering enrollment information from parents/guardians
- suggested forms to use at enrollment
- the importance of analyzing enrollment data to build programming

We showed how the enrollment process is critical for making data-driven decisions that will guide the development of programming for ELs. In the next chapter, we describe the different types of programming that are typically implemented for ELs and how these should be adjusted to accommodate ELs at the beginning stages of English language development.

RESOURCE 3.1
Student Oral Language Observation Matrix

Student's Name: _____ Grade: _____ Language: _____

Translator: _____ Date of Observation: _____

Based on your observation, indicate, with an X in the appropriate box, the level that best describes the student.

Level	1	2	3	4	5
A. Comprehension	Cannot be said to understand even simple conversation.	Has great difficulty following what is said. Can comprehend only "social conversation" spoken slowly and with frequent repetitions.	Understands most of what is said at slower-than-normal speed with repetitions.	Understands nearly everything at normal speed, although occasional repetition may be necessary.	Understands everyday conversation and normal classroom discussions without difficulty.
B. Fluency	Speech is so halting and fragmentary as to make conversation virtually impossible.	Speech is usually hesitant, with the student often forced into silence by language limitations.	Speech in everyday conversation and classroom discussion is frequently disrupted by the student's search for the correct manner of expression.	Speech in everyday conversation and classroom discussions is generally fluent, with occasional lapses while the student searches for the correct manner of expression.	Speech in everyday conversation and classroom discussions is fluent and effortless, approximating that of a native speaker.

Level	1	2	3	4	5
C. Vocabulary	Vocabulary limitations are so extreme as to make conversation virtually impossible.	Misuse of words and very limited vocabulary make comprehension quite difficult.	Frequently uses the wrong words; conversation is somewhat limited because of inadequate vocabulary.	Occasionally uses inappropriate terms and/or must rephrase ideas because of inadequate understanding of vocabulary.	Use of vocabulary and idioms approximates that of a native speaker.
D. Pronunciation	Pronunciation problems are so severe as to make speech virtually unintelligible.	Very hard to understand because of pronunciation problems. Must frequently repeat in order to make self understood.	Pronunciation problems necessitate concentration on the part of the listener and occasionally lead to misunderstanding.	Always intelligible, though one is conscious of a definite accent and occasional inappropriate intonation patterns.	Pronunciation and intonation approximates that of a native speaker.
E. Grammar	Errors in grammar and word order are so severe as to make speech virtually unintelligible.	Grammar and word order errors make comprehension difficult. Must often rephrase and/or restrict self to basic patterns.	Makes frequent errors of grammar and word order, which occasionally obscure meaning.	Occasionally makes grammatical and/or word order errors, which do not obscure meaning.	Grammatical usage and word order approximate those of a native speaker.

Source: Developed by the San Jose Area Bilingual Consortium with revisions from the Bilingual Education Office of the California Department of Education.

RESOURCE 3.2
Home Language Survey

Please answer the following questions for each child attending [name of school]. Your answers will help us in creating the best possible educational program for your child.

Student's Name (please print): _____ Date: _____

Date of Birth: _____ Place of Birth: _____

Home Address: _____

School: _____ Grade: _____

Home Language Questions	Answers
1. What language did your child first understand or speak?	
2. What language do you or others use most often when speaking with your child at home?	
3. What language does your child use most often when speaking at home?	
4. What language does your child use most often when speaking with other family members?	
5. What language does your child use most often when speaking with friends?	
6. What language(s) does your child read?	
7. What language(s) does your child write?	
8. At what age did your child start attending school?	
9. Has your child attended school every year since that age? If no, please explain.	☐ Yes ☐ No
10. Would you prefer oral and written communication from the school in English or in your home language?	☐ English ☐ Home language Name of language: _____

Signature of Parent/Guardian: _____ Date: _____

Please return completed form to the School Office.

Source: Zacarian (2011).

RESOURCE 3.3
Identification, Annual, and Transition Assessment
Findings and Recommendations

Student's Name: _____ Gender: M F Grade: _____

Student Assessed By: _____ Date Tested: _____

Assessment Type: ☐ New Student ☐ Annual ☐ Exit/transfer from Program

Summary of Listening and Speaking (Include name of the assessment, scores, and summary of findings.)

_____

_____

_____

Summary of Reading and Writing (Include name of the assessment, scores, and summary of findings.)

_____

_____

_____

Placement Recommendations

☐ Does not need English language education services
☐ Needs English language education services
☐ Reclassify as former English language learner

ESL Level for Identified English Learners (check box that applies)

(See next page for description of levels.)
☐ 1 Starting   ☐ 2 Emerging   ☐ 3 Developing
☐ 4 Expanding   ☐ 5 Bridging and Reaching

Clarification in Native Language Needed:

☐ No ☐ Yes If yes, language needed: _____

Description of Levels for Identified English Learners

Level 1, Starting: Total beginner. Cannot communicate in English at this time. Student has very limited or no understanding of English and does not use English for communication. Responds nonverbally to simple commands, statements, and questions. As oral comprehension increases, will begin to imitate verbalizations of others by using single words or simple phrases. At the earliest stage, constructs meaning from text primarily through illustrations, graphs, maps, and tables.

Level 2, Emerging: Understands basic interpersonal conversation when spoken to slowly and with frequent repetition. Speech strongly influenced by native language. Understands phrases and short sentences. Can communicate limited information about simple, everyday routine situations by using memorized phrases, groups of words, and formulae. Uses selected simple structures correctly but still systematically produces basic errors. Beginning to use general academic vocabulary and familiar everyday expressions. Errors in writing are present that often hinder communication.

Level 3, Developing: Has learned enough vocabulary and language to speak with peers and teachers. However, has not yet developed the competencies in English needed to perform ordinary academic activities. Understands more complex speech but still may require some repetition. Uses English spontaneously but may have difficulty expressing all thoughts due to a restricted vocabulary and limited command of language structure. Speaks in simple sentences that are comprehensible and appropriate but that are frequently marked by grammatical errors. Proficiency in reading may vary considerably. Is most successful constructing meaning from texts for which student has background knowledge upon which to build.

Level 4, Expanding: Language skills are adequate for most day-to-day communication needs. Can communicate in English in new or unfamiliar settings but has occasional difficulty with complex structures and abstract academic concepts. May read with considerable fluency and is able to locate and identify the specific facts within the text. However, may not understand texts in which the concepts are presented in a decontextualized manner, the sentence structure is complex, or the vocabulary is abstract or has multiple meanings. Can read independently but may have occasional comprehension problems, especially when processing grade-level information.

Level 5, Bridging and Reaching: Has native or near-native use of spoken English. Emphasis needed on reading and writing with a focus on form and meaning in academic areas. Can express himself or herself fluently and spontaneously on a wide range of personal, general, academic, or social topics in a variety of contexts. Is poised to function in an environment with native-speaking peers with minimal language support or guidance. Has a good command of technical and academic vocabulary as well as idiomatic expressions and colloquialisms. Can produce clear, smoothly flowing, well-structured texts of differing lengths and degrees of linguistic complexity. Errors are minimal, difficult to spot, and generally corrected when they occur.

Source: Zacarian (2011).

RESOURCE 3.4
Interview of Parent/Guardian and/or Newly Identified
English Learner Central Valley School District

Newly identified English learners and/or their parents/guardians should be interviewed to assist in building an effective instructional program. The following questions are intended for this purpose. The interview may be conducted with parents/ guardians, parents/guardians and their child, or the student. The person conducting the interview should complete this form.

Date of Interview: _____

Student Name: _____ Grade: _____

Interviewer: _____ Position: _____

Who was interviewed: (☐ parent/guardian ☐ parent/guardian with student or ☐ student)

Interpreter (if applicable): _____

1. How long has [name of student] attended school? _____

If student was enrolled in a prior school, ask Questions 2–7. All parents/guardians and/or students should be asked Questions 8–9.

2. What schools has your child attended? Where are these schools located, and what dates did he or she attend?

   a. School Name: _____

   Location: _____ Dates Attended: _____

   b. School Name: _____

   Location: _____ Dates Attended: _____

   c. School Name: _____

   Location: _____ Dates Attended: _____

3. Is more than one language used to communicate in the student's prior school(s)? ☐ Yes ☐ No If yes, what are the language(s)? Also, please describe when and how these are used.

4. What do classrooms in the student's prior school(s) look like (typical student–teacher ratio, arrangement of desks, print on walls, etc.)? (Try to get a feel for the school.)

5. Please describe the school day (length of day, daily schedule, etc.).

6. In what ways do parents/guardians participate in the student's prior school?

7. Were the student's teachers concerned about his or her progress? If yes, please describe the concerns.

8. Do you have any particular concerns, including academic, social, and disciplinary?

9. What is the highest level of education that you and your spouse have completed?

☐ Elementary

☐ Middle or Junior High School

☐ High School or Equivalent

☐ Community College

☐ Vocational School

☐ 4-Year College/University

☐ Professional Graduate Degree

Source: Zacarian (2011).

4 Selecting Models of Instruction

Margarita, a new immigrant from Colombia, entered the fourth grade at a well-known dual language school in Florida. Her reading, science, math, and social studies classes are taught in Spanish. Even though her school's 1,500 students are from low-income families who often struggle to get their economic needs met, the students' test scores are among the highest in the city. Margarita is below grade level in Spanish reading and math, and she receives extra support in these areas. Her English as a second language (ESL) instruction is tailored to her beginning level of English language development. She is making excellent progress in her new school, where she has been welcomed and assigned to classes that are appropriate to her language needs.

Eduardo is a new immigrant from Guatemala who entered the eighth grade at a middle school in a small town in Delaware. He has been identified as a beginning learner of English and has been placed in an eighth-grade ESL pull-out program that meets every day for 40 minutes. Eduardo is overwhelmed in his content area classes, because his subject area teachers do not know how to work with a beginning-level English learner (EL). Also, most of his teachers speak very little Spanish. His ESL class includes 15 students who are at varying stages of English language acquisition from beginning to advanced. Eduardo cannot understand most of what is occurring in his ESL class.

Although Eduardo's ESL teacher is dedicated to her students, the large range of English language development levels in the class makes meeting the needs of beginners very difficult. We feel that beginning language learners can benefit from working with ELs who have a range of abilities in an ESL class. However, we also feel that they need direct instruction in a class that is designed specifically for them.

We devote this chapter to presenting different models of instruction for ELs, including the ones described above in the scenarios. These include models that promote (1) bilingualism and biliteracy, (2) transitioning students from learning in their home language to learning in English, and (3) using English to learn English (structured immersion). Each model includes two components: English language development, commonly referred to as ESL, and academic content learning such as math, science, and social studies. For the purpose of this chapter, we present these models as they apply to beginning learners of English.

PROGRAMS THAT PROMOTE BILINGUALISM AND BILITERACY

Several program models used by school districts to teach ELs, such as dual language, two-way bilingual, and bilingual maintenance programs, are based on a belief in bilingualism and biliteracy. These models are ideal when a school district has a critical mass of ELs from the same language group. In these programs, ELs continue to learn in their home language as they learn English. They develop language proficiency in two languages by receiving instruction in English and in their home language (Soltero, 2004). There is wide variation in how instruction is provided among bilingual immersion programs (Goldenberg & Coleman, 2010; Soltero, 2004). Some programs provide instruction for children in Grades PreK–2 as a 90/10 model, with 90% of instruction in the native language and 10% in English. The amount of time that instruction is provided in English is gradually increased until it is 50%. Optimal bilingual immersion programs have a balance of the number of ELs and fluent speakers of English in a class.

Programs that promote bilingualism and biliteracy are a growing choice for school districts that want bilingualism for all of their students. As we saw with Margarita in the dual language program, classes comprise native speakers of English and native speakers of a minority language. Table 4.1 lists the various program types and their alternate names and characteristics.

The goal of these program models is a high level of academic achievement in both languages. However, programs vary in the amount of time that they teach in each language and which grade levels they serve (E. E. Garcia, 2005). The Center for Applied Linguistics (1999) offers a list of dual language and two-way bilingual programs. Figure 4.1 describes a typical course of study for ELs during the first year.

Table 4.1 Programs That Promote Bilingualism and Biliteracy

Program Type	Known as	Characteristics
Maintenance bilingual	Developmental Enrichment	All participants are ELs
Bilingual immersion	Dual language Two-way Double immersion Two-way immersion	Participants are ELs and native speakers of English

Figure 4.1 Year 1 for a Beginning Learner in a Bilingual Program

Year 1
Language arts in a student's home language
Math, science/technology, and social studies in a student's home language
Language arts in the target language (e.g., English for English learners and Spanish for fluent speakers of English)

EARLY EXIT OR TRANSITIONAL BILINGUAL PROGRAMS

There are two types of transitional bilingual education (TBE) programs: early exit and late exit. In early-exit models, the goal is not bilingualism and biliteracy, but to move ELs as quickly as possible from learning in their home language to learning in English (Soltero, 2004). This method is most common in kindergarten and first grade, with instruction in the native language phased out after 2 or 3 years in the program (Gersten & Woodward, 1995). In some instances, beginning ELs are relegated to an all-English learning environment before they are able to learn academically in English.

In late-exit models, students continue to develop in their home language after they have become proficient in English. All TBE models require a critical mass of students who speak the same language. During the first year, late-exit TBE programs may look very similar to bilingual-biliterate models for beginning learners of English.

State regulations often govern the structure of providing bilingual education and require a specific number of the ELs that speak the same language (e.g., 20). Schools should consult with their state department of education to determine when a bilingual model is required. If your district is required to develop a bilingual program, we recommend a bilingual-biliterate model.

STRUCTURED IMMERSION MODELS

Structured immersion models include lessons that are specifically designed and delivered for students to learn English as they learn content. This is commonly called *sheltered immersion content*, ESL, or *content-based ESL* (Echevarria, Vogt, & Short, 2004; Soltero, 2004). These programs can, but do not always, include bilingual support or clarification in the native language whereby instruction is delivered in English and explained in the primary language as needed. Sheltered English is often used when there are speakers of many different languages and not enough of any one language to implement bilingual programming. Table 4.2 provides information on this type of model. Figure 4.2 describes what a typical first year in such a program would look like.

Each of these program models is based on a belief that students can learn best when teachers plan and deliver lessons for English language development and content learning. Indeed, guiding principles of English language education are that students must develop academic language and academic content knowledge to be successful in school, and the two processes are interrelated (Collier & Thomas, 2009; Egbert & Ernst-Slavit, 2010; Gibbons, 2009; Gottlieb, Katz, & Ernst-Slavit, 2009).

It is the our experience that even well-crafted programs need to be modified for beginning ELs. One of the most popular methods of structured immersion is the Sheltered Instruction Observation Protocol (SIOP;

Table 4.2 Programs That Are Primarily Taught in English

Program Type	Also Known as	Goal	Characteristics
Structured immersion Sheltered Immersion	Pull-out Push-in content-based ESL ESL pull-out ESL ESL push-In	To develop the ability to learn solely in English in mainstream classrooms conducted entirely in English	Model taught entirely in English with limited support in the native language

Figure 4.2 Year 1 for a Beginning Learner in a Structured English Immersion Model

Year 1
ESL
Math, science/technology, and social studies taught in English using structured immersion

Echevarria, Vogt, & Short, 2004). While SIOP and other sheltered instruction (SI) methods may work well with intermediate-level English learners, they may not necessarily meet the needs of beginners unless specific attention is given to students at this language level.

Let's look at a typical fourth-grade sheltered social studies lesson taught by a teacher in Oregon who has been trained to use SIOP. Mrs. Weber is teaching a unit on Pilgrims and wants her students to compare the lives of children living in the Plymouth colony in 1621 to their own lives. She writes that objective on the board: "Compare the lives of Pilgrim children in 1620 to your lives in 2012." She first reviews previously taught lessons on the chores that Pilgrim children had to do and the homes they lived in. She also reviews a list of jobs that was brainstormed by the whole class at the beginning of the unit. Unit vocabulary from a word wall is also studied. Students are separated into pairs. Each pair is given a large Venn diagram with the labels "Children in 1621" and "Children in 2012." Students are instructed to complete the Venn diagram with their partner.

Although this is a very straightforward lesson with fine support for emerging ELs, it is too difficult for beginners. Why? Beginners do not have the cultural background knowledge to make sense of the history behind the lesson. Also, the linguistic demands of the lesson are too difficult for beginners. Here are some ideas on differentiating this SIOP lesson for beginners. Beginners could do the following:

- label picture of vocabulary pertinent to the lesson
- develop a timeline using significant dates from their lives
- communicate ideas through drawing and labeling pictures
- fill in the Venn diagram using photographs of jobs/chores that children do in 2012 and drawing pictures of children doing chores in 1621

Translating a lesson, while helpful, does not provide the type of explanation and activities that students need to learn. Beginning ELs must grasp the concept of the lesson being taught and actively engage in activities that help them apply the content and concepts. We suggest that beginning ELs receive separate ESL instruction designed especially for them, even when they are placed in a SIOP class.

ESL INSTRUCTION

So we have three models of English language education: bilingual-biliterate, transitional bilingual education, and structured immersion. ESL is an important component of each of these models, but it can also be a freestanding program. Generally, there are two types of ESL instruction: pull-out and push-in, or collaborative teaching.

ESL Pull-Out

Although we favor bilingual or structured immersion models, ESL pull-out programs are prevalent, especially in schools with low numbers of ELs. In ESL pull-out, students leave the general classroom each day to attend an ESL class. Even though curriculum for an ESL program could be based on the subject that is taught in the general education classroom, pull-out programs do not usually duplicate instruction.

Pull-out models have many complexities. ESL pull-out classes are often 30 minutes in duration. This amount of time is insufficient, especially for EL beginners (Duke & Mabbot, 2001). ESL programs often include students from a variety of language backgrounds, grade levels, and ability levels. Pull-out classes commonly occur during content instruction, resulting in ELs being taken away from critical subject matter instruction. Typically, ESL teachers do not speak the languages of their students, and support is not provided in students' native languages. This might be occurring because language support is viewed as prohibitively expensive and impractical. Another complexity is that ESL teachers often use an eclectic approach that is not tailored to ELs in any one grade, ability level, or English language development level. In these situations, it is common for teachers to (1) organize theme-based instruction from science, social studies, and/or reading curricula that addresses the most common grade levels represented among ELs or (2) provide a fragmented program of English language development that is not targeted to the diverse language and academic learning needs of ELs. In addition, most general classroom and secondary subject matter teachers have had little preparation to teach ELs, especially those at the beginning stages of English language development (Hollins & Guzman, 2005).

Another important complexity that needs to be addressed is the reality that ESL pull-out classes often occur in shared rooms, noisy cafeterias, corners of school libraries, hallways, converted storage rooms and closets, small crowded spaces, or under stairwells (Haynes, 2008). Judie visited a school with a well-known ESL program where two teachers shared a room. One taught K–1 ELs, and the other Grades 2–6 ELs. This was not an ideal teaching situation for either teacher. In addition, many ESL pull-out teachers are often required to travel to two or more schools each day. Ms. Castle is a perfect example. She is an itinerant ESL teacher from Pennsylvania who travels to four schools and teaches a total of 20 students spanning Grades K–12. Seven of the students are beginners. The remainder are at different levels of English language development. Ms. Castle organizes her ESL program in the trunk of her car. Some of her classes have students that span four grade levels. In addition, Ms. Castle teaches in whatever space she can find and in a different location every day. Often, teachers forget that she is coming, and Ms. Castle spends an inordinate amount of time traveling from one classroom to another to gather her students. Like most itinerant teachers, the challenges that she encounters have to do with more than securing the space that she needs to teach and the time that she needs to adequately provide instruction. She is also unable to function as a consistent source of support and information for her students, their families, classroom teachers, and specialists. Most important, we have observed that all too often itinerant ESL teachers are not included on child study teams when their ELs are referred for special education evaluations. This team, consisting of a school psychologist, a learning disabilities teacher/consultant, and a school social worker, often makes decisions about an EL's education without adequate knowledge of second language acquisition and what a high-quality learning environment for ELs should look like. It is important that ESL teachers have time in their schedule to attend these meetings when one of their students is involved. In our opinion, it's essential.

When students and ESL pull-out teachers are marginalized in the ways that we have described, it sends a powerful message to ELs, their families, and the school that educating ELs is not an important priority (Haynes, 2008). ESL pull-out programs need to have more support from administrators so that they may help create as seamless a program as is possible. ESL programs are also dependant on ESL teachers having time to support classroom and subject area teachers as well as meet with parents. They also need adequate space. Figure 4.3 lists the minimum requirements for an ESL program that serves beginning ELs.

Figure 4.3   Minimum Requirements for ESL Programs for Beginning ELs

✓	ESL instruction for at least 90 minutes or two class periods every day that is targeted to the unique language development needs of EL beginners
✓	Grouping of ELs by grade and proficiency level; classes should not span more than two grade levels
✓	A limit of two schools per ESL teacher
✓	Instructional space that is comparable to the general education settings in the building with similar size student populations
✓	Schedules that allow ESL teachers time meet and collaborate with general education teachers, child study teams, and parents
✓	Professional development in second language acquisition and methods for teaching ELs listening, speaking, reading, and writing

Push-In or Collaborative ESL

In a collaborative or coteaching setting, the ESL teacher "pushes into" the general education classroom to collaborate with the general education teacher. Coteaching involves two credentialed professionals who are partners in the instruction of a content area lesson. One professional is usually a classroom or subject area teacher and the other is a certified ESL teacher.

Over the past 10 years coteaching has become more popular as school districts search for ways to best serve the needs of their ELs. ESL teachers, who are actually implementing these programs, report many tensions with this model. Many ESL teachers do not believe that this model is beneficial to their students and often feel that it is forced on them (McClure & Cahnmann-Taylor, 2010).

Let's consider Cecilia Gonzalez's experience as a coteacher at an elementary school in a suburban town in Wisconsin. Ms. Gonzalez worked as an ESL pull-out teacher for 7 years, bringing her students to her own classroom for a 40-minute ESL class. Three years ago, her school switched to a push-in model of ESL with the stated intention of providing a more inclusive educational model. Mrs. Gonzalez now coteaches with five different teachers each day. She has no common planning time with any of them. One of her coteachers turns the whole class over to her for part of the period and uses the time as a prep period for herself. In several other classes, Ms. Gonzalez teaches at the back of the classroom with a few ELs while the classroom teacher works with the majority of the students. In another collaboration, she roves around the room to help students who do not understand the instruction. One of her coteachers, a veteran math teacher, does not allow Ms. Gonzalez to speak in Spanish. Thankfully, there is one classroom teacher who meets with Ms. Gonzalez at lunch to co-plan science lessons for her classroom.

As we can see from this description, Ms. Gonzalez and most of her students have been relegated to the fringes of the classroom. In true coteaching models, the classroom teacher contributes subject matter knowledge and the ESL teacher offers depth of knowledge about second language acquisition and teaching practices with ELs. Push-in or coteaching models work well when teachers are given time to co-construct lesson plans and code-liver them. These are crucial components of successful coteaching models (Haynes, 2007a; Honigsfeld & Dove, 2010). Honigsfeld and Dove (2010) contend that scheduled time for planning instruction is essential to the success of a collaborative partnership. To promote this successfully, coteachers require professional development.

Let's look at an example of a coteaching model in which teachers collaborate successfully. Mrs. Hansen is a fifth-grade science teacher, and Mrs. Barrett is the ESL teacher who is pushing into her class. They are planning a unit of study on the planets, and they meet regularly to plan their unit goals and objectives. They agree on the key content goals that will be taught to the students and plan together how the unit will be cotaught. Mrs. Hansen teaches the content goals to the whole class, and Mrs. Barrett focuses on teaching the language of content (Honigsfeld & Dove, 2010). Both teachers direct their attention to the beginning learners of English in their class as well. Beginners are pretaught the necessary vocabulary to support the language of the lesson, including concrete nouns, verbs, and descriptive adjectives. The ELs in this class clearly benefit from the coteaching model. They are not isolated from the rest of the class; rather, they are intentionally included in it.

Coteaching at the High School Level

Coteaching works well at the middle and high school levels as well. Let's look at a model that combines the best of sheltered instruction and coteaching. At Lincoln High School, a large suburban school in a suburb in New Jersey, science and social studies classes are designed for the needs of ELs from 12 different language backgrounds. Let's look at a 10th-grade American History class at this school. Two teachers are instructing 15 beginning- to intermediate-level ELs. An ESL teacher, Mr. Henderson, and a certified social studies teacher, Ms. Fox, teach the class. The content for this class is sheltered, and language is differentiated for the needs of the ELs in the class. Mr. Henderson plans modified lessons for the beginners and preteaches the vocabulary and key concepts during their beginning-level ESL class. (All the students in the class are also assigned to one or two periods of ESL depending on their language needs.) Let's look at a lesson that Mr. Henderson and Ms. Fox teach from a unit on U.S. government. The whole class learns about people participating in the government, including detailed descriptions of their functions (Board of Regents of the University of Wisconsin System, 2011). Beginning ELs work with partners to match pictures of people in the different branches of government and what their function is (e.g., president, Supreme Court justices, Senate and House leaders).

Another ESL teacher at Lincoln High School coteaches a biology class that all ELs take during their first or second year in the United States. Typical beginning ELs at Lincoln High School takes five courses during their first year. This includes two ESL classes, sheltered social studies and science classes, and an elective in the arts or in world languages. They receive English credit for their two ESL classes and can receive world language credit by passing a test or completing a project in their native language.

No matter what kind of program your district decides to use, we advocate for an ESL program of instruction that is tailored for beginners at their level of academic development and chronological age. We also believe that professional development is a critical component and have devoted Chapter 9 to this important area. Beginning ELs also need to have support in their native language, including instructional materials. Fortunately, Spanish materials are available and a wide variety of resources in additional languages can be found on the Internet. We provide further information on this in Chapter 6.

NEWCOMERS WITH LIMITED PRIOR SCHOOLING

In addition to the models described earlier, there is a model that is targeted specifically for school-age ELs who are new to the United States and have significant educational gaps. School districts nationwide are recognizing the unique needs of this population and are providing programming that is targeted for them. The goal of most of the programs for these students is that once they acquire the skills that are needed, the students will exit into the model types that we described earlier in this chapter at the beginning level of English language proficiency. Commonly referred to as *newcomer programming*, these programs reflect the following goals and objectives:

- help students acquire beginning English skills
- provide some instruction in core content areas
- guide students' acculturation to the school system in the United States
- develop or strengthen students' native language literacy skills (Short & Boyson, 2012)

Effective newcomer models, according to Short and Boyson's (2012) research findings, include the following:

- flexible scheduling of courses and students
- careful staffing plus targeted professional development
- basic literacy development materials for adolescents with reading adaptations targeted specifically for ELs
- content area instruction to fill gaps in education
- extended time for instruction and support (e.g., after school, Saturday, and summer programming)
- connections with families and social services
- diagnostics and monitoring of student data
- transition measures to ease newcomers into regular school or beyond high school

Let's look at 15-year-old Amir, who is currently in a newcomer high school. Amir recently moved to New York City from Sudan, where he had very little formal schooling. After meeting with the school's intake registrar, Amir was placed in a *newcomer program* intended to help him acquire some beginning conversational skills in English, help his entrée to the United States, provide support in his native language, and help him learn core content information. After Amir has completed the newcomer program, he will move to the school district's regular ESL or bilingual program. In Chapter 7, we speak more about students like Amir who have come to the United States with limited or interrupted formal education.

SUMMARY

In this chapter we discussed many different types of programs of instruction for beginning ELs:

- dual language, two-way, and bilingual maintenance programs that promote bilingualism and biliteracy
- programs whose goal is to transition students from native language to English in a relatively short period of time
- various structured immersion models in which instruction is in English, including sheltered English as well as ESL push-in and pull-out models
- programming for secondary students with significant gaps in their education

We have shown how essential it is for beginning ELs to be given specialized instruction to meet their needs. We described modifications for sheltered English and ESL pull-out and push-in models to better serve the English language development of beginning ELs.

In Chapter 5, we describe the challenges that parents of ELs face when their children enter school in the United States. We discuss the importance of building partnerships with families of beginning ELs by establishing a welcoming environment and empowering parents by giving them a voice in their child's education.

5 Strengthening Family–School Engagement

Bella's parents moved from the Dominican Republic to Georgia, where Bella was born. While they are excited for her to begin school, they worry about her lack of English. Bella's grandparents care her for while her parents work, and she has had very little exposure to English. They are looking forward to meeting with her kindergarten teacher, Miss Carlson, to learn about how Bella is doing in school. Miss Carlson sent Bella home with a note for her parents confirming the date and time for the parent–teacher conference. When the parents arrive with their preschooler and Bella in tow 45 minutes after the appointed time, Miss Carlson is not sure how to tell them that she cannot meet with them as she has another parent conference scheduled. When she tries to explain that they are late for the conference, she is not sure that they understand the importance of being on time. Miss Carlson later complains to her colleagues that perhaps Bella's parents don't care about their daughter's education.

Valentino is a sixth-grade student who recently moved to Iowa from Sudan with his parents. During the first snowstorm in December, his school has a 2-hour delayed opening. Valentino and his parents are not aware of what delayed openings are and have little knowledge of Iowa's winter weather. On the day of the delayed opening, Valentino walks to school wearing a light jacket and sneakers, with no gloves, scarf, or hat. By the time he reaches the front door, he is wet, freezing, and crying. When the staff arrive 2 hours later and see Valentino, they begin to think about the steps that they can and will take to keep this from happening in the future.

Think about these scenarios as you reflect on how the families of the English learners (ELs) in your school district are welcomed and come to understand the implicit rules and processes that routinely occur in school. How do you rate your school? We suggest that you complete the *Rate the Intake Procedures of Your School* activity in Resource 5.1 found at the end of this chapter. As we discuss the importance of parent engagement, continuously reflect on ways that you think you might strengthen your partnerships with parents.

BUILDING PARTNERSHIPS WITH FAMILIES OF BEGINNING ENGLISH LEARNERS

Many educators are not familiar with their diverse population of ELs, and simultaneously many parents of ELs do not understand the routines and practices of their child's school and the expected and often implicit role that parents play in their child's education (Henderson, Mapp, Johnson, & Davies, 2007). Unfortunately, this often leads to students and their families being in the margins of their school (Lawrence-Lightfoot, 2003). While all parents love their children and want them to do well in school, parents of ELs, especially those new to the country, have to do double the work of fluent speakers of English who are familiar with U.S. public schools. Why? School has so many implied rules of being and acting that are far from transparent. Learning the norms, rules, and routines of what occurs in a given community and developing the strategies and skills needed to negotiate them is a difficult, if not impossible task.

According to Lawrence-Lightfoot (2003), the absence of this implied knowledge and practice can and does prevent parents from engaging in their child's school, even on the smallest of levels. We fully agree with these claims and, at the same time, recognize it as a two-way street. Like many parents of ELs, we believe that many educators and educational leaders often lack knowledge of the norms, rules, and routines of what occurs in the homes and communities of their ELs. Further, this lack of knowledge often prevents parents and educators from working together to provide the best possible education for students. Educators' lack of familiarity about the social, cultural, linguistic, and economic differences poses unique challenges for them to actively engage with ELs and their families. However, we strongly believe that partnerships can be forged in a positive and long-lasting way.

The term *partnership schools* (Henderson et al., 2007) reflects an intentional belief that families are rich and critical resources. In practice, this means that parent engagement is essential to student success. It is important to note that when we use the word *parent* in this chapter, we are referring to the family community that is raising and caring for children. This can include a grandparent, aunt, uncle, caregiver, or other guardian. It is the person—or, in many cases, people—acting as the parent community of the child. Drawing from Henderson et al. (2007), building parent partnerships consists of these essential elements:

- understanding barriers
- establishing a welcoming environment by building relationships
- addressing differences
- building connections with learning
- supporting advocacy and sharing power

UNDERSTANDING BARRIERS

Parents of beginning ELs face seemingly insurmountable obstacles when they try to understand the education that their child is receiving. They often do not speak English, are unfamiliar with U.S. educational systems, may not be literate in their home language, and do not share the norms of the mainstream culture. A common dilemma, frequently seen as an insurmountable barrier, is that many ELs and their families live in poverty ("A Distinct Population," 2009; Goldenberg & Coleman, 2010). In addition to working more than one job, parents of beginning ELs are often unfamiliar with their new community and its services, such as public health, housing, medical, and dental care, and may not have transportation.

Engaging parents of beginning ELs in the education of their children is essential to students' success in school. It calls for us to think anew about the ways in which every parent can be involved in the school and community, especially in terms of accessing the services and activities that are available for ELs' families. While we want the parents of our beginning ELs to "buy into" our purpose, learn our school culture, and support our programs, we must also want to build partnerships with them and help them engage in the community as a whole.

In this chapter, we look at the essential elements of laying a firm foundation for empowering parents of beginning ELs in their children's education.

ESTABLISHING A WELCOMING SCHOOL ENVIRONMENT BY BUILDING RELATIONSHIPS

Parent engagement begins by learning how to converse *with* parents of beginning ELs in meaningful ways rather than speaking *at* them (Ferlazzo, 2011). An important first step in this process is to learn as much as we can about our parent communities. In some schools, this includes visiting the homes of students. In others, it might include having families enjoy a cup of tea at the school for the sole purpose of engaging them in a welcoming social experience. In addition, because so many ELs live in poverty, preparing for parent partnerships can and should include being aware of the social services that are available and securing information about them in the languages of our parent communities. One welcoming ESL teacher or office staff member cannot do this job alone. It must be a whole-school effort that is led by administrators with buy-in from all school staff.

Bilingual bicultural translators should be an essential component of any of these welcoming activities for beginning-level ELs and their families and should also be an integral part of meeting with families. While translators are essential, it is important to treat parents with respect and dignity. Think of what it would be like to be a parent who is dependent on a translator to communicate with your child's school. What would you want to occur? We suggest the following:

- finding translators who have depth of knowledge about school practices and the school's EL parent communities,
- providing translators with training about the type of translation activities that are needed,
- lengthening meeting time to ensure important back-and-forth flow of information, and
- remembering to look at and speak with the parents when you are communicating with them.

Supporting parents of beginning ELs should include providing ample opportunities to help them understand the routines and practices that occur in their child's school. Here is a small list of elements that are important to fully explain:

- the school calendar, including planned holidays, delayed openings, closings, and early dismissals
- the time that school starts and ends
- weather-related closings, delays, and so forth
- how to report that a child will be absent and how to write an excuse after the absence
- afterschool activities available for their child
- student code of conduct
- means for parent involvement, including parent–teacher organizations, bilingual advisories, and so on

When a new family walks into your school, knowledgeable school office or intake personnel should greet them warmly. It is important for office personnel to know that many parents from different countries and cultures do not share the same greeting ritual of shaking hands. However, a warm attentive smile and very prompt welcome is important. After all, this is a family's first experience with the school, and it should be a positive one. Ask the family to pronounce their and their child's full name, and learn to pronounce it correctly. This begins the important reciprocal process of building relationships and, importantly, the personnel can then help members of the school community properly pronounce and say the name of the new child and their family. It is also important to note that in some cultures the name is said in a different order than is used in the United States. The family name may go first and the given name second. Two-part first names are also common in many cultures and may appear to be a first name and a middle name. It's important to learn whether a child generally uses both parts of a two-part name. Some cultures use two family names. They both should be used in U.S. schools. It's important to avoid the temptation to Americanize an EL's name or create a nickname. Of course, if the student offers a nickname or an Americanized version of his or her name, we should accept it. Saying the name right isn't necessarily easy, but it's a first means of showing interest and investment in building relationships with new families and students.

Hallways should reflect the diversity of the school. Families should be able to see signs in diverse languages and pictures from various countries. A large world map in the main hallway would allow parents to show school personnel where they are from. Flags from different countries can also create a welcoming environment. School personnel and teachers should learn a few words in the languages of the students. If you can't find information about the language of a newly arrived EL, ask parents or students to teach you a few words. One principal we know recorded words of greeting in various languages on her cell phone so that she could refer to them when greeting the parents of her ELs.

Mrs. Taylor, a librarian in a school in Connecticut, created a section of bilingual books in her library. She invited parents from various language backgrounds to help her choose the books that were included. What amazed everyone involved in the project was that native-English-speaking students also checked these books out of the library. Mrs. Taylor's library became a regular stop on her school principal's school tour so that parents of beginning ELs, community members, and others could meet EL parent volunteers and see the range of multilingual books.

ADDRESSING DIFFERENCES

Yukiko Nakamura is a third grader from Japan whose family moved to the United States due to her father's work. While Mr. Nakamura speaks English, he works long hours and leaves Yukiko and her mother alone for most of the week. Yukiko has been very unhappy in school. Although Mrs. Nakamura's English is quite limited, she makes an appointment with her daughter's teacher, Mrs. Creighton, to discuss Yukiko's difficulties with the other students in the class. At the meeting, she tearfully tells Mrs. Creighton about how the other students are making fun of the lunch that Yukiko brings to school. She uses her hands to demonstrate how they hold their noses. In Japanese culture, it is part of the mother's job to ensure that children have all that they need to succeed in school. The Japanese *bento* is a work of art with beautifully arranged and freshly made Japanese food (Hays, 2009). Mrs. Nakamura is upset by the reactions of her daughter's classmates to the lunches she has so carefully prepared. After Mrs. Nakamura explains the problem, Mrs. Creighton responds, "Well, would it be possible for you to make her a peanut butter and jelly sandwich?"

Mrs. Creighton's response demonstrates, albeit unintentionally, an absence of knowledge about Yukiko's culture and a lack of understanding about the depth of culture shock that the family is experiencing. Mrs. Nakamura is overwhelmed with her responsibilities in a culture that she does not understand, and she has little support outside of her husband, who works long hours and leaves the caregiving for his child almost entirely to his wife. She doesn't know what a peanut butter and jelly sandwich is or how to find the ingredients for it. Coming to school to speak to her child's teacher is also unusual and out of character for her. Her husband asked a colleague at work what to do when his daughter was being teased and was told to go into the school. This information was passed on to his wife, who followed these plans.

One of the reasons that schools fall short when involving parents of ELs in school is the lack of familiarity that teachers and school administrators have with immigrant parents. This lack of knowledge often leads to miscommunication and, while unintended, insufficient sensitivity and empathy. We have heard teachers claim that the parents of ELs do not care about how their children are doing in school. Many also tell us that parents should learn English and be familiar with what the school expects. Because ELs are enrolled in general education classrooms (and many are enrolled in these for the majority of their school day), it is important for us to consider the concerns of general classroom and subject area teachers toward ELs. According to Schmidt (2000) and Valdes (2001), general elementary and secondary classroom teachers have many productive tensions about teaching ELs, including

- lack of time to meet the needs of ELs in the classroom,
- intensification of workload when ELs are enrolled in class,
- feelings of not having adequate knowledge to successfully teach ELs, and
- negative feeling about working with ELs.

It is our experience that when teachers have time to learn about their students, it often leads to a positive disposition toward teaching ELs. For some of these teachers, it may be the result of

- experience or course work in foreign languages and multiculturalism,
- course work in second language acquisition,
- positive personal experiences with world cultures and people, and
- contact with ELs with diverse backgrounds.

However, we have found that we cannot expect that all teachers will have had these life experiences. While one of the most pressing mandates of school districts is to develop respect for the various linguistic and cultural representatives in the school, this has to be done in an intentional way by providing administrators, school secretaries, custodians, cafeteria workers, and teaching staff with multiple experiences to develop the knowledge that is needed to work with ELs effectively and successfully.

Many ELs feel lost during the first year and rely on their teachers and other school personnel to help them navigate through the school day as smoothly as possible. If we understand that we are likely to have students from diverse social, economic, linguistic, cultural, and world experiences, we must view diversity as a strength and an asset as opposed to a barrier. To do this means that we have to begin from a place in which we believe that every parent loves and cares for his or her child and that we all want children to do well in school. It also must reflect a strong sense of commitment to understand students' families and their cultural ways of being and to build relationships that are mutually respectful and caring.

BUILDING CONNECTIONS WITH LEARNING

We often send students home with academic work that some parents cannot support. Then we complain that parents are no help. There are ways that parents can participate in their child's education. These involve changing the paradigm to one in which academic learning is connected with students and their families' social, cultural, and world experiences (Zacarian, 2011). When we value these interconnections and believe strongly in building strong, caring relationships with our students and families, it can greatly help us to link school with home, especially with families of beginning-level ELs. The following are some important elements to consider in creating these connections.

The beginning of the school year is a common time in which new students enroll in school. However, ELs can enroll at any time. This is especially true for students that come from countries that operate on a different school calendar. As we know, many parents of ELs are not literate or have limited literacy, have experienced trauma, and live in poverty. School can be much more welcoming if social activities are a part of the entrée of parents. It is possible to connect these well to what is happening in school.

Routines such as Open House and parent conferences should be preceded by social events such as potluck suppers where every parent can participate. At the same time, family activities such as these can also be connected to what students are learning (Henderson et al., 2007; Zacarian, 2011). Parents of beginning ELs can benefit greatly from these socializing activities for many reasons. It helps bring communities together, welcome new families, and, most important, get schools to be welcoming and inviting.

Helping parents get involved in school activities is critical for building partnerships. A powerful example of this is a semester-long project in which two educators supported their students to create digital stories that portrayed the immigration experience of a family member or friend (National Writing Project, 2009). In the project, collaborative groups of students conducted interviews, videotaped them, and used this material to create an extraordinary film that was shown to families and friends at the end of the semester. The project is a superb example of how families can be an integral part of an educational program when schools consider them as powerful assets.

A second example is the ESL Literacy Club for ELs and their families that was created by Mrs. Schnee, an awarding-winning kindergarten ESL teacher in New Jersey. Mrs. Schnee started the club by inviting parents to their child's kindergarten ESL class 1 day a week for 6 weeks. During this class time, parents observed Mrs. Schnee as she conducted a read-aloud and emphasized a different reading comprehension strategy each week. Each family received a copy of the book that was read. Although Mrs. Schnee taught the class in English, she helped her students' families understand how to apply this information to reading in their home languages. She continues to provide this activity. Information and tips on how to help children read is also regularly posted on her website. Knowing that many of her students' families are newcomers to the United States, she routinely takes them on field trips to the local bookstore and shows them how to choose books for their children. Parents of ELs who participate in Mrs. Schnee's program are treated respectfully as assets and are supported to feel and be comfortable. They don't hesitate to ask questions and contribute to their child's education. In addition to the Literacy Club, Mrs. Schnee and other highly effective teachers continuously think of new ways for helping parents of beginning ELs become involved in their child's school. They do this by taking the time to learn about their parent communities and infusing what they learn into their family engagement work.

An important consideration in this type of thinking is to evaluate the purpose of ritualized meetings such as Open House and parent conferences and make them explicit and transparent because many parents of ELs do not know the purpose of such events and how they are expected to behave during them (Haynes & Zacarian, 2010; Zacarian, 2011).

Part of the professional development of classroom and subject area teachers, guidance counselors, and other school personnel should focus on how to hold productive meetings with the parents of beginning ELs in order to build meaningful communication and relationships and to learn about differing cultural beliefs. As often as possible, we should consider what it would be like if we were new to the community and school so that we can plan ways in which we will work well with our parent communities.

SUPPORTING ADVOCACY AND SHARING POWER

Each of the elements that we have discussed thus far—understanding barriers, establishing a welcoming environment by building relationships, addressing differences, and building connections with learning—are all targeted to help parents be actively engaged in their child's schooling. They involve a commitment to be in constant communication with families in order to ensure that they are welcomed and comfortable in the school and that we are advocating for them to be as involved as they can.

We understand that there are many reasons why parents may not have been much of a presence in their child's school. It may not be a cultural norm to do so. Parents may not have transportation or child care for younger siblings. They may feel embarrassed by their lack of English or inability to read the notices that come home, even those that have been translated. Parents may be unwilling to miss work because they are afraid (for good reason) to lose their jobs. We need to find ways to overcome these obstacles. When parents do not come to school meetings, we should not assume that they are not interested in their child's education. An oral invitation issued in their native language may encourage parents to come to school. Overcoming hurdles might include using a bilingual parent phone tree. When a new parent enrolls his or her child, the bilingual phone tree is activated to helpfully explain what is occurring. Schools might also think of ways to provide transportation and child care so that parents can come to school more easily. In one school district, a local business leader asked the principal of a middle school if she could recommend a bilingual Asian parent to sit on a local hospital board. When the principal took this request to teachers and administrators in her school, no one could think of a single parent that would be suitable for the job. This was a wake-up call for the school community. They realized that they had failed to engage parents in leadership roles in the school. It became their mission to find ways to encourage parents to become school leaders.

BILINGUAL PARENT ADVISORY COMMITTEES

In many states, schools with programs for ELs are required to form a bilingual parent advisory committee. Holding group meetings with parents/ guardians and extended families of beginning ELs at the start of the school year is a good way to organize parent committees. Many districts have ELs who represent more than one and even many languages. In these instances, it might seem impossible to hold a parent or family meeting in the native languages represented among this population. However, this should not be an insurmountable barrier. Most communities include bilingual speakers of the languages that our parent communities speak. It is very important to make connections with the various churches and local agencies to tap into the available community resources for this much-needed activity. Not only do translators help parents/guardians and extended families learn about their child's school; they also provide them with the essential opportunity to meet other parents and engage with the community.

Meetings in English must be very carefully planned. The overall objective of holding a meeting for the parents is twofold: (1) to help them feel and be welcomed into the school community and to help educators feel and be able to communicate with families and (2) to help parents understand a school's culture and procedures to engage parents in the school community and to help the school community learn about the parent community.

Parent advisory committees composed of members from ELs communities are essential for helping schools and parents work together. For example, a school may want to explain its homework policy, or the school nurse may want to talk about health issues. We want to set the stage for a welcoming and nonthreatening environment.

It's also helpful to send a reminder letter the day before a meeting or, better yet, to have a volunteer make phone calls to parents in the home language. It is also helpful to think through the meeting plans and send parents information about what is planned to help provide the information that is needed for participation. Think about all of the school customs that we take for granted. Our colleagues can help us make these meetings more meaningful. Here are some of the topics to cover at a parent advisory meeting:

- the local school district's program for ELs and its benefits
- state and federal laws regarding programs for ELs and parents' rights
- criteria for exiting students from an English language education program
- clarification of school procedures and culture
- state testing
- report cards, study habits, and parent–teacher conferences
- information about serving on a parent committee, becoming a school volunteer, and working on a program in which their child will be participating

It is always helpful to include the school principal as well as a community liaison or social service worker in these meetings. Translators should be secured in advance of the meeting and are essential for helping parents communicate. The translator may be a bilingual parent or someone employed for the meeting. We have found that many parents of beginning ELs find it very hard to speak in front of an audience and feel more comfortable writing and/or speaking in their own language in small groups.

HOME VISITS TO INVOLVE PARENTS OF ENGLISH LEARNERS

Home visits are common in many parts of the country. If they are not popular in your area, they might be something your school should investigate. Proponents of home visits tell us how much they learn from this experience. One teacher told us a story about a parent that she visited. The parent expressed a desire to learn English but did not have child care or transportation to the adult school where the English classes were held. The school collaborated with parents to establish free English classes at a church that was located right in their neighborhood. Money was raised to pay a teacher, and the school found high school volunteers to provide child care.

Another way to connect with parents is to hold meetings at local churches or community centers. School partnerships with local churches and community-based agencies can be very beneficial when a school is working to engage parents in their child's education. Many of these meetings occur on Sunday, the only day of the week most parents do not work.

BILINGUAL PARENT VOLUNTEER PROGRAMS

Many urban school districts have bilingual parent liaisons on their staff. We suggest that schools in suburban areas with smaller EL populations start a bilingual parent volunteer program. A fine place to start is by recruiting a few key bilingual parent volunteers who speak English well. They do not have to be parents of ELs and they do not have to be available during the school day. It is helpful, however, to have a few parents who are available during the school day. The purpose of these key volunteers is to disseminate information to parents who do not speak English and are unable to understand the communications from the school.

Everyone gains from the participation of bilingual parent volunteers in a school. The school benefits from an increase in the quality of communications with the parents of beginning ELs. Parents feel more comfortable in the school and often develop friendships with the teachers they help (Haynes, 2007b).

The bilingual parent volunteers in Judie's school in New Jersey translated a handbook written for beginning ELs into Korean, Japanese, and Chinese. Bilingual parents originally brought the idea of the handbook to Judie and the school principal. The final handbook covered all of the school programs, including PTA activities, afterschool programs, and traffic safety rules for dropping children off at school. These handbooks were given to new Japanese-, Korean-, and Chinese-speaking parents when they registered at the school.

Another very important function of bilingual volunteers is to establish a phone chain for parents of beginning ELs belonging to the same language group. This chain can be used for emergency school closings, delayed openings, and early dismissals. It can also be used to remind parents of school activities such as a parent meeting or a school science fair. It provides another way for schools to keep in touch with parents of beginning ELs. This kind of chain in Valentino's school would have prevented him from having the upsetting experience of being sent to school early when a delayed opening had been called. If phone calls to parents for school closings are automated, have parent volunteers record the message in the home languages of the students in your school.

If you have a few bilingual parent volunteers who are at home during the day, they can help with new arrivals during registration and giving a tour of the school. It is a way that a school can introduce new families to the school and support enrollment communication.

SUMMARY

In this chapter, we discussed how engaging families should be an important priority for any program with beginning ELs. While building family partnerships involves adapting the activities that may already be occurring in your school and creating new ones, it is worth the effort. We talked about essential elements of building connections with parents, including establishing a welcoming environment by building relationships, addressing differences, building connections with learning, supporting advocacy, and sharing power.

In Chapter 6, we talk about teaching ELs during their first year of school. We outline ways that schools can engage these students from the first month of school and discuss how culture shock impacts learning, the role of native language support, and how to communicate with beginners. We also discuss how to use bilingual aides, classroom buddies, and bilingual parent volunteers in school and provide key strategies for teaching beginning ELs.

RESOURCE 5.1
Rate the Intake Procedures of Your School

Look at the following descriptions. Check the box on the left side for practices your district already does and the box on the right side for things you will begin doing to improve your school's readiness for ELs.

Occurs	Procedure	Will Occur
	School secretaries or intake personnel receive training to greet new families, minimize anxiety, and understand culture shock.	
	Teachers and administrators have received professional development about the cultures of the ELs in the school.	
	Bilingual interpreters routinely help with registration and explain school practices to parents.	
	Bilingual interpreters are available after school so that teachers can meet with parents.	
	Parents are included in the school community through translated notices, school calendars, lunch menus, events, and other important school information.	
	Mainstream students have been sensitized to cultural differences and practice tolerance and cooperation. Self-esteem and school morale are high.	
	Videotaped greetings and school tours are available for newcomers in their native languages.	
	Beginning ELs are placed in age-appropriate grades/classes.	
	School personnel know how to place students with no school records.	
	Students with no or interrupted prior schooling are given immediate literacy instruction based on their needs and beyond typical ESL classes.	
	Information about different cultures is readily available to teachers.	
	Classroom teachers receive advance notice of an EL's arrival to prepare seating and texts, assign a buddy, and create a welcoming atmosphere.	

Occurs	Procedure	Will Occur
	Bathroom doors have international male/female symbols painted or posted.	
	ESL and/or bilingual teachers' schedules include time to support classroom teachers and train aides, parents, and student volunteers.	
	Appropriate materials are available to newcomers for classroom use.	
	A percentage of media funds is spent for books and dictionaries in the native languages of the student body as well as easy readers and picture books suitable for ELs.	
	Newcomers' native languages are respected; maintenance and growth in native language literacy and cognition are formally encouraged.	
	School walls, decorations, and labels reflect an awareness and welcoming of newcomers and include students' home languages.	
	A list of all people in the school who speak each language represented by its ELs is kept in the main office in case of an emergency.	

6 Teaching Beginners

Aditya, a new fifth-grade student who recently arrived from India, is aggressive toward his classmates on the school playground. He is very frustrated about his inability to communicate and lashes out when he doesn't understand what is being said. One day, the only other Hindi-speaking student in his class was absent and Aditya couldn't speak to his classmates at all. He became very upset, ran from the classroom, and left the school. His anger and unhappiness were apparent, and his teacher felt that there was "something wrong" with him beyond the language barrier.

WHAT IS CULTURE SHOCK?

No discussion of English learners' first year of school would be complete without talking about culture shock. As educators and educational leaders, the more we and our students do to help English learners (ELs) cope with the challenges that they face, including the anxiety that they might feel as they enter a new learning environment, the more positive their experience will be. While anxiety can manifest itself in a myriad of ways, it leads to insecurity and a barrier to learning (Krashen, 1985). Many ELs experience these behaviors and dispositions. Conversely, the more positive the experience, the more open ELs are to learn.

Moving to a new school can be difficult for any student. For students who have to learn a new culture and language, the change can be traumatizing. If beginning ELs are coming from a different country for the first time, they will experience the trauma of a new culture, often referred as culture shock. Culture shock can dramatically affect a student's first year in a U.S. school. Aditya's orientation to school in the United States was especially hard. The school principal placed him in a classroom where there were no other speakers of Hindi. Aditya's parents felt he would learn English much more quickly if he was not able to speak Hindi in school. As a result, he was in a classroom without any native language support. What might have happened if Aditya had been placed in a classroom where there were more Hindi-speaking students? We might surmise that his culture shock would not have been so severe. However, students like Aditya are not alone. Many come to school with little support in their native language and are enrolled in classrooms where instruction is in a language that they do not understand.

Teachers, administrators, and other school personnel must also realize that not all beginning ELs will suffer from culture shock in the same way. The spectrum varies from withdrawn and passive to aggressive. The greater the difference between the new culture and the students' primary culture, the greater the shock (Haynes, 2005b). For example, a student moving from Mexico to Arizona, where there are many Spanish speakers, may not experience culture shock in the same way as a student moving from Sudan to Minnesota. ELs who are new to the United States have often left behind family members, friends, teachers, pets, and entire ways of being and acting within their home communities. Their parents may be unable to help them because they are also suffering from culture shock.

STAGES OF CULTURE SHOCK

In educational settings, researchers and practitioners recognize four of stages of culture shock (Brown, 1994). As educators, we need to be aware, or be made aware, of these stages and how they can influence the behavior of newly arrived ELs:

1. Honeymoon or euphoric stage

2. Rejection or culture shock stage

3. Integration stage

4. Assimilation or adaption stage

Stage 1—Honeymoon or Euphoric Stage

The honeymoon stage is often characterized by initial excitement about learning a new language and culture. Students at this stage may feel euphoric about their new adventure, and this euphoria can last from one day to several months. This is the time for school communities to learn about the backgrounds of their ELs and provide a welcoming and understanding environment. It is also an important time to avoid overwhelming ELs with unrealistic amounts of work.

Stage 2—Rejection or Culture Shock Stage

Some ELs enroll in school during this stage, which is characterized by potentially rejecting the new culture and feeling frustrated because they cannot communicate or negotiate in it. While beginning-level ELs begin to see the differences between the American school culture and their home culture, they cannot participate in it and thus find themselves continually stressed. They may feel overwhelmed by what they need to learn and are bombarded with "unfamiliar surroundings, unreadable social signals and an unrelenting barrage of new sounds" (Haynes, 2005b, p. 2). They may also seem sleepy, irritable, disinterested, or depressed. Some students may become aggressive and act out their frustrations, as Aditya did in the opening scenario of this chapter. They may also avoid learning English, socializing with their classmates, and doing schoolwork.

What are the implications for our classrooms and school communities? We need to show patience and understanding. We also have to accept that what beginning ELs are feeling is normal and set realistic expectations and goals that are obtainable. Although we should set boundaries for students like Aditya to help keep them from acting out, we need to do this calmly, patiently, and empathetically. We must find adults or others who speak the same language as new ELs so that we can support their entrée into school. Beginning ELs need to be reassured that what they are feeling is normal and that the adults in the school are going to help them.

Stage 3—Integration Stage

In this stage, ELs start to deal with differences between the old and new cultures. This is a vacillating stage when students begin to learn to integrate their own beliefs with those of the new culture. Some ELs will start to replace their old values with new ones and may reject their home culture and language. Others will begin to find ways to exist with both cultures. During this stage, we need to support the maintenance of, and show respect for, the native languages of our ELs. Yes, we may want our students to learn English and American culture, but we do not want to do this to the detriment of their first language and culture. Our goal should be to develop bilingual and bicultural students.

Stage 4—Assimilation or Adaptation Stage

During this stage, ELs will enter and thrive in the general education classroom. They will either accept and assimilate American culture and their home culture or adapt to the new culture and reject their home culture. Ideally, students will be successful in negotiating the culture of school while continuing to value their home culture.

Once school personnel learn to recognize culture shock and develop methods to support students, ELs will be more able to participate in their classrooms. Showing patience and maintaining a welcoming classroom helps beginner ELs advance to Stage 3, where they are ready to work, more quickly.

SUPPORTING ENGLISH LEARNERS IN CONTENT AREA CLASSROOMS

Let's look at Aditya's academic program during the first year of school. His program includes one English as a second language (ESL) class per day. In addition, he has been placed in general education content area classes for math, science, and social studies. Although all of his teachers want to help him, none have received training in teaching ELs so they do not feel confident in their decision making.

How can Aditya's teachers help him? We believe that ELs should be engaged in meaningful instruction throughout the school day. They need to be involved in their content areas classes from the first months of school, even though their ability to participate may be limited. For this to occur successfully, all teachers must be language teachers and understand second language development. Aditya's teachers need to plan and deliver lessons that meet his level of English language development. Classroom and content area teachers also need resources for providing information in a student's native language. To help beginning ELs during the first year of school, the following strategies and tools are important to consider:

- bilingual programming or, when this is not available, bilingual support in content area classes
- programs to provide bilingual buddies and cross-grade tutors
- bilingual parent volunteers

Bilingual Support in Content Area Classes

Bilingual support in content area classes is an asset to subject matter teachers and beginning ELs. We feel that beginning learners of English need this type of support in core subject areas. Bilingual support personnel need to be carefully selected. While bilingual bicultural support is greatly helpful, it is essential that personnel speak, read, and write in an EL's first language and have solid command of English. They must also have the appropriate academic and social vocabulary and be able to communicate well with teachers, parents, and school administrators.

It is important that people providing bilingual support have an understanding of the subject area information that is being taught. Their job in the classroom is not just to translate; it is also to explain the concepts. Bilingual support is much more effective in classrooms where the teacher differentiates instruction for ELs in the class. The teacher needs to decide what content should be taught to the ELs depending on their English language level. It is not reasonable to expect bilingual support personnel—whether volunteer, aide, or tutor—to translate all the material that is being covered by native English speakers.

Bilingual Buddies for English Learners

Bilingual buddies can be terrific assets when a beginning EL first arrives. During the first months of school, the bilingual buddy can explain in the EL's native language, with meaning, what is occurring. It's important to support buddies to work with ELs and to reward students who take this job seriously. This helps ELs feel comfortable in the general education classroom, and the buddy gains in self-esteem.

It is also a good idea to rotate buddies and to use classmates who don't speak the student's native language. These classmates can help newcomers socially. They can support students during non-class time, such as lunchtime, on the school bus, at recess, and during other social times that are critical for newcomers. In middle and high schools, buddies can be great assets by taking new students to their classes in order to help them navigate from one class to the other. By rotating buddies, teachers can involve the whole class in the success of ELs.

When Eduardo and Vanessa first came to the United States from Colombia and entered the second and third grades, respectively, their ESL teacher arranged for former ELs from the same language background in the fifth grade to tutor them during lunchtime. The older students were excited to share their knowledge with Eduardo and Vanessa. They used teaching methods that had helped them learn English and developed visuals for common words. They planned lessons and worked diligently to help their "students." They also explained school rules and helped the newcomers negotiate the new culture. These fifth-grade students received a commendation from the principal for their efforts (Haynes & Zacarian, 2010).

Bilingual Parent Volunteers

Song Jae is a Korean middle school EL who has enrolled in school in Connecticut. In addition to his beginning-level ESL class, Song Jae has been placed in a U.S. History class that is studying the Civil War. Unfortunately, though his teacher is trying her best to deliver lessons that are at Song Jae's beginning level of English and use strategies that are geared for him to understand the content, he is overwhelmed in his new environment. Parent volunteers would like to help Song Jae. They find a book written in Korean about the U.S. Civil War and discover websites via Google Korea that include support in this subject area. This critical Korean-language support makes a huge difference in Song Jae's ability to understand the content and participate in his U.S. History class. It also helps his teacher to more effectively plan and provide lessons that Song Jae can understand.

USING TECHNOLOGY AND THE INTERNET

It is extremely important to find native language resources for beginning ELs. These include age-appropriate bilingual dictionaries, story and literature books in students' home languages and at their reading levels, and web 2.0 resources that support English language and content development. Websites such as Google Mexico and Google Korea are also helpful, as are sites that provide translations into different languages, such as Simple English Wikipedia or online dictionaries with translations. Although online electronic translators do not necessarily provide accurate translations from English to various languages and vice versa, they can provide some helpful support on the topics that ELs are studying. We would not hesitate to use handheld translators for helping our beginning ELs.

There are also online phrasebooks in different languages that can be downloaded for free at from the Cultural Orientation Resource Center. Windows to the Universe is a science website that provides information on science topics at different levels of English and in Spanish. Pumarosa is a good site for teaching basic concepts in English to Spanish speakers. Schools that do not have adults on staff who speak the languages of ELs might work to develop a districtwide and/or community resource of bilingual parents, students, and community members as well as Internet resources. Corwin also hosts a website (www.corwin.com/beginningells).

MATERIALS AND RESOURCES
FOR BEGINNING ENGLISH LEARNERS

Technology is an important resource for beginning learners of English. A computer or iPad (or other tablet) with an Internet connection and a set of earphones can greatly support ELs in accessing numerous websites that provide opportunities to practice English and read materials in their native language. It is always helpful to find content that has been adapted for ELs. Texts and supplemental materials for ELs are a fine resource. Well-illustrated or photographed nonfiction books that have controlled vocabulary are also a great resource. Many textbook series have strands for ELs. It is important to preview these to assess their usefulness for beginning ELs as they may be targeted for ELs at a more advanced stage of proficiency. ESL teachers can be a great help in determining the usefulness of course materials and supporting general classroom and subject matter teachers in choosing from among these resources.

TEACHING ESSENTIAL BASICS

Initial lessons should be designed to enable beginning-level ELs to navigate their way through the school, including

- where the bathrooms, lockers, nurse's office, guidance office, main office, cafeteria, art and music classes, gym, bus areas. and other special area classrooms are located;
- how to buy lunch, tell the school nurse when they are sick, find the school bathrooms, and ask directions;
- the names of teachers, the school nurse, the school secretary, guidance counselors, the principal, and custodians;
- orientation to school procedures: hall passes, late passes, behavior in hallways, rules for the cafeteria and playground, sneakers for gym, and raising hand in class;
- school life vocabulary.

Teaching everyday expressions and what they mean is essential for teachers of beginning learners of English. These help students to become familiar with the school environment and develop social links with their peers, teachers, and community. It is essential to teach concrete vocabulary, including objects or actions that can be demonstrated. Resources 6.1 provides a school life vocabulary list that is intended to support beginning learners of English in developing familiarity with the basic terms, words, idioms, and phrases that are needed during the first months of school.

EIGHT KEY STRATEGIES FOR TEACHING CONTENT

General grade-level and subject matter teachers need to become both language and content teachers of ELs. This involves thinking carefully about the strategies needed to do so successfully. Let's look at sixth-grade science teacher Mr. Hurley as he teaches a unit on volcanoes. First, he selects essential information on different types of volcanoes, how they are formed, and how they create new land. He identifies the key vocabulary (terms, words, idioms, and phrases) that his students will need in order to demonstrate their understanding of this content. His beginning ELs are responsible for just the key concepts in the chapter, not for reading a journal written by an author who had been present during an eruption of Mount St. Helens. Mr. Hurley is using the same book that is used by native- English-speaking students, but he is modifying the content for beginning ELs. He supplements the book with online resources. He begins to think about the ways in which he will effectively educate the beginnings ELs in his class. What does he do?

Box 6.1 lists key strategies that we have found work well when teaching ELs across the content areas (Haynes & Zacarian, 2010).

BOX 6.1   Eight Key Strategies for Differentiating Instruction for English Learners

1. Provide information that beginning ELs can understand.

2. Link new information to students' background knowledge.

3. Determine key concepts for the unit, and define language and content objectives for each lesson.

4. Modify vocabulary instruction for ELs.

5. Use cooperative learning strategies.

6. Modify testing and homework for ELs.

7. Differentiate instruction for ELs with technology.

8. Teach thinking skills to ELs.

---

1. Provide Information That Beginning English Learners Can Understand

Language is not "soaked up." Beginning-level ELs will not understand what is being taught unless modifications are made. In schools where there are no bilingual programs, ELs are often assigned to general education classrooms and spend most of their day in this environment. It is especially critical for them to receive comprehensible information from their teachers and classmates. Comprehensible input is provided by the use of visual supports for a lesson, differentiated instruction, and native language materials.

Let's look more closely at Mr. Hurley's class. The beginning ELs are studying diagrams found online of the parts of the volcanoes and the different types of volcanoes. While the rest of the students are learning with a grade-level textbook, his ELs are acquiring information on three types of volcanoes online at Windows to the Universe. Mr. Hurley has set the site at the beginner level in English, and his Spanish-speaking ELs read the material on the website in their native language first. Chinese- and Arabic-speaking students are reading material on volcanoes in their native language on Wikipedia. As they read, they label the different types of volcanoes. They also watch the eruption of a volcano on TeacherTube. Mr. Hurley uses Thinkfinity to make simple drawings available for his beginners.

Mr. Hurley is also using graphic organizers and diagrams to help his students visualize the content that he is teaching. He has created these with actual photographs of volcanoes to illustrate the content in an authentic way. In the center of the graphic organizer, he has written *Volcano* and placed an accompanying photograph of a volcano next to it to depict the word. He has placed three outer circles around the center photograph. Each contains a photograph as well. These provide an authentic visual of the three types of volcanoes, which he has also labeled. He knows that graphic organizers are important tools for his beginning ELs. Drawing from Hyerle, Curtis, and Alpert's (2004) research using specific organizers to depict different types of thinking skills, Mr. Hurley knows that consistency in the type of organizers that he uses is extremely helpful for his beginning-level ELs.

Mr. Hurley also likes to use short trade books that are well illustrated with controlled English for his beginning ELs. These students are reading National Geographic's *Volcanoes*, by Catherine Stephens. They are also reading a nonfiction picture book on volcanoes that Mr. Hurley found in the school library. He has made sure that the book covers are not too juvenile.

Mr. Hurley also has a variety of bilingual dictionaries in his classroom that are targeted for ELs and include pictures of the volcano content that they are studying. When his students are finished with the volcano unit of study, he knows the importance of saving all of the modifications that he made, as he knows how valuable they will be for his current and future students.

2. Link New Information to Students' Background Knowledge

Instruction should be linked to the students' personal, cultural, and world experiences. Building these connections is more than linking new information to what has been previously taught. For example, Mr. Hurley calls upon the bilingual support personnel that are available to him and asks them to call parents so that the parents talk about volcanoes or other natural disasters in that occur in their home countries and/or stories about people they know that might have experienced a volcano or natural disaster. He knows that this type of parent–child interaction helps his students build connections between the content and their lives.

3. Determine Key Concepts for the Unit and Define Language and Content Objectives for Each Lesson

Mr. Hurley writes the key concept for the volcano unit of study in very simple English. He does this in the form of a question to help spark his students' interest (Wiggins & McTighe, 2005). His key question for his volcano unit is "How do volcanoes change the earth's surface?" Additionally, he knows the importance of beginning each lesson by writing a content or learning objective in very simple language on the board and leaving it there throughout the lesson. The content objective describes what he wants his students to learn. Today's content objective is "What are three types of volcanoes?" Mr. Hurley knows the importance of referring to his unit and content objective at each transition during class (Haynes & Zacarian, 2010). For example, he reviews the unit and day's content objectives at the beginning of the lesson and refers to them again after he models the activities that his students will do in class. He also revisits them at the end of the lesson to support a discussion about whether the objectives were met.

While Mr. Hurley does a great job of creating simply worded objectives and refers to these to support his students' study of the content, he also provides them with support in their native language. Same-language buddies and/or support staff translate this activity for beginners.

Mr. Hurley also writes language objectives for his unit. For the lesson about the three types of volcanoes, EL beginners are asked to find action words in the text and draw a picture to demonstrate each word. For the ELs in his class who are not literate in their native language, Mr. Hurley provides more instruction. He models what action words or verbs are and guides students to find their four examples.

4. Modify Vocabulary Instruction for English Learners

During Mr. Hurley's volcano unit, students begin the lesson with pictures of the Earth's mantle, crust, and magma. This is followed with games and puzzles using the words to provide students with vocabulary practice. Mr. Hurley also uses a graphically organized word wall with supported pictures to display the key vocabulary and phrases that his beginning ELs need in order to communicate. He has native English speakers use a

Smartpen, which is a digital pen that can speak when reading notes written on special paper. Students write the vocabulary words and a simple definition so that beginning ELs can take a word off the wall and listen to the pronunciation and a simple definition of illustrated words. Mr. Hurley does all of these activities because he knows that ELs require direct instruction of new vocabulary. This is crucial for beginning ELs. Concrete nouns and simple verbs, function words, adjectives, adverbs, and conjunctions must be taught for beginning ELs to learn the language of content and begin and be able to communicate in it. Providing beginning ELs with multiple opportunities to practice the proper pronunciation and learn the meaning of new words is a constant in Mr. Hurley's class. He knows that these students need much more exposure to new words and phrases than do their English-fluent peers. Tying new vocabulary to prior learning in much the same way that we suggested tying key concepts to a student's schema is important. Visuals of new vocabulary words reinforce meaning.

5. Use Cooperative Learning Strategies

In Mr. Hurley's class, cooperative groups conclude the volcano unit by creating a poster using Glogster. The beginning ELs in his class gather pictures from the Internet for the poster. Mr. Hurley does not lecture at all. He knows that lecture-style teaching excludes beginning ELs and others in his classes. Working in small groups is especially beneficial to beginning ELs. It provides a fine space in which to have an authentic reason to learn key concepts and use academic vocabulary. Beginning ELs should be grouped with at least one same-language peer, if possible. Roles or jobs in cooperative learning groups can be modified for beginners. They can gather supplies, draw pictures, and look for illustrations online. These are the roles that Mr. Hurley assigns successfully to his beginning ELs.

6. Modify Testing and Homework for English Learners

Mr. Hurley's homework assignment for his beginning ELs is to speak with their families to learn if anyone experienced a volcano or natural disaster. In class, he observes his beginning ELs carefully to ensure that the activities he assigns are being done successfully. This type of formative assessment helps him make needed adjustments as the lesson is occurring. Mr. Hurley also knows that he has to modify the assessments that he will administer to his beginning ELs. Alternative types of assessment that he knows to choose from include having his students provide an oral and/or physical response (e.g., act it out) as well as their drawing or illustrating a response.

7. Differentiate Instruction for English Learners With Technology

As we have mentioned throughout this chapter technology is a wonderful resource for beginning ELs and their teachers, and Mr. Hurley uses it throughout his lessons. Not only can teachers access information in their students' native languages, but there are a plethora of ways that web 2.0 tools and applications for iPods, iPads, and other devices can be used to increase opportunities for beginning learners of English to practice listening and speaking skills. Many educators who have used iPods, iPads, and podcasts have commented that their beginning ELs have much shorter silent periods and become more enthusiastic about learning than do ELs who did not have access to technology. Other web 2.0 tools encourage ELs to read and write. We have noticed a great increase in the time spent on writing when beginning ELs began using a computer to write and post blog entries. Beginning ELs were much more willing to attempt writing and to make corrections to their work.

The nation's new digital divide is between schools, communities, and people that have high-speed Internet and those that do not (Crawford, 2011). This reflects the disparity between those who cannot afford computers and high-speed Internet service and those that can. Dr. Anete Vasquez, professor at Kennesaw State University, engages her preservice teachers in a writing assignment to understand the digital divide. She requires her students to take public transportation to the local library, where they are required to use the library's computer and Internet access to do the assignment. Her students experience firsthand what it is like to wait in line to sign up for a 30-minute session and complete the assignment within the allotted time. Most find that their time is up before they can complete the assignment. For example, if three other people are signed up for a computer session, Dr. Vasquez's student has to wait 1.5 hours until being able to get back onto the computer. Dr. Vasquez has found this assignment to be a powerful learning experience for her students. Because so many ELs live in poverty and may attend schools and live in circumstances where they have limited access to computers and high-speed internet, it is important for us to find solutions that eliminate these barriers.

8. Teaching Thinking Skills to English Learners

Mr. Hurley also supports his students in understanding the thinking skills that are needed to complete the tasks in his lessons. He recognizes the importance of this for many reasons. For example, bilingual staff helped him learn that some of the ELs in his class did not have the grade-level academic language skills that they needed in their native language or in English to be successful in his class. We end this chapter with a description of thinking skills as they apply to beginning-level ELs, and we draw from Bloom's taxonomy in doing so (Krathwohl, Bloom, & Masia, 1973).

Level I: Knowledge. In general terms, this level of thinking requires students to think for information purposes. For beginning learners of English, it is possible to provide questions that require concrete information. Students can be supported to respond through body language, pictures, photographs, drawings, and realia. Answers to questions at this level can generally be found in the text, and beginning ELs can be successful in responding to this task. Here are some questions about volcanoes from Mr. Hurley's lesson:

1. Name the layers of the Earth.

2. What are the names of the three types of volcanoes?

3. Label the different parts of a cone volcano.

Level II: Comprehension. This level of Bloom's Taxonomy shows that students have understood the content area information and can interpret it. Beginning ELs can be asked to compare, contrast, illustrate, and classify oral questions and graphic organizers such as Venn diagrams and T-charts. Here are some questions that Mr. Hurley asked to test his ELs level of comprehension:

1. Compare a composite volcano with a shield volcano using a T-chart.

2. Make a chart showing the characteristics of the three types of volcanoes.

Level III: Application. At this level, beginning ELs are being asked to apply what they have learned to solve problems. These students need scaffolding and word banks to complete activities at this level. Here are two questions Mr. Hurley asked so that his ELs could employ this level of thinking:

1. Make a list of ways that volcanoes change the Earth.

2. Explain how the Earth's crust has cracks in it.

Level IV: Analysis. This is a difficult level for beginning ELs because they will not have the language and vocabulary in English to explain their analysis of ideas. Beginning ELs who are literate in their native language should be able to complete tasks at this level in their native language. Tasks in English need to be teacher directed and heavily scaffolded. Here are some examples from Mr. Hurley's class:

1. Look at the map of the Earth's plates. Why are so many volcanoes located on the Ring of Fire?

2. Find information on five volcanoes that have been active during the past 5 years, and find their location on the map of the Earth's plates.

Level V: Synthesis. Beginning ELs need teacher support and scaffolding to synthesize information; they don't have the skills in English to perform tasks associated with this type of thinking without such support. Tasks at this level can be completed in students' native language. ELs may be able to choose, combine, create, design, develop, imagine, make up, predict, solve, and change in very simple English. Mr. Hurley had beginning ELs work with a group on these tasks:

1. Make a model volcano.

2. Draw a diagram of how volcanoes helped form the Hawaiian Islands.

Level VI: Evaluation. Questions at this level of Bloom's Taxonomy can be modified so that the language is simplified but the task remains the same. Beginning ELs can learn to give opinions. Here are some questions from Mr. Hurley's class that beginning ELs would be able to answer with some scaffolding by the teacher:

1. What would the earth be like if there were no volcanoes?

2. How would you feel if your family was going to move to a country where there is an active volcano?

SUMMARY

The first year at school in the United States is key to the academic success of beginning ELs. For these students to become an integral part of the school community, we as educators and educational leaders need to ensure that they have a positive educational and social experience (Haynes, 2005a).

In Chapter 7, we discuss how to engage ELs who have experienced trauma. We demonstrate how war, natural disasters, and personal trauma affect ELs' performance in school. We also show how schools can develop trauma-sensitive practices while supporting social, language and literacy, academic, and thinking skill development within a whole school–whole classroom context.

RESOURCE 6.1
Vocabulary for Beginning English Learners in School Settings

While this is not a complete list, it is intended to support teachers in providing key words for beginning learners of English. The list should be expanded to include the words and language that is essential for particular contexts.

Body Parts		Colors
head	foot	red, yellow, blue, orange, green, purple, white, black, brown, gray
eyes	toes	
ears	legs	**Dates**
nose	thigh	
mouth	knees	calendar
neck/throat	waist	day, month, year
arm	stomach	days of the week
shoulders	elbow	months of the year
elbow	hand/fingers	holidays

Emotions	Greetings	Names/Titles
happy/glad	Hi/hello	Miss, Mrs., Ms., Mr., Dr.
surprised	How are you?	students' names
angry	Fine/I'm fine	teachers' names
scared/afraid	How's it going?	first name
nervous	What's happening?	last name
sad	See you later	principal, vice principal
upset/worried	Goodbye	nurse

Responses	Classroom	
yes	desk	bookcase
no	seat/chair	pen/pencil
maybe	clock	crayon/marker
I don't know	white board	ruler
I don't understand	flag	eraser
please repeat/say again	pencil sharpener	scissors

School	Classes	Clothing
name of school	ESL	shirt/t-shirt
address of school	math/algebra/geometry	pants/jeans
school office	science	skirt/dress
nurse's office	social studies/history	jacket/coat
hallway	language arts/English/writing	shoes/sneakers/boots
lockers	music	sweater
gym	physical education/gym	scarf/gloves
bathroom/restroom	art	cap/hat

Cafeteria/lunchroom	Instructions	
lunch	arrange	stop
lunch line	bring your	listen/look
tray	name	line up
salad bar	count/count off by	take out your
food	put/name	write
fork/knife/spoon	draw	label
plate/bowl	hand in/pass in	raise your hand
napkin	show	be quiet/no talking

Nurse's Office	Gym/PE	Library
scale/weigh	ball (basketball, etc.)	books
thermometer/temperature	game	computer
icepack/Band-Aid	run/jog/climb	librarian
hurt/sick	field (football, soccer)	magazine/book
headache/stomachache	basketball court	check out/return
I hurt my	gymnastics	overdue
I have a pain in my	score	borrow

Restroom/Bathroom	Grades	Safety Signs
toilet/toilet paper	check/checkmark	caution
sink/water	correct/incorrect	beware
soap	answer/response	don't walk/walk
flush	A, B, C, D, F	fire alarm/fire drill
paper towel	pass/fail	danger
wash your hands	incomplete	poison

Directional		
across	before/after	left/right/middle
around	bottom/top	center/edge
at	front/back/behind	near/next to
away	in back of/in front of	on/off
on/in	up/down	above/below
between	forward/backward	east/west/north/south

Family	Math	Money
mother/mom	numeral/number	cent/penny
father/dad	plus/add	nickel/dime/quarter
sister/brother	equal/equal to	dollar bill
grandfather/grandmother	divide/multiply	five/ten/twenty dollars
aunt/uncle	less than/more than	change
cousin	add/subtract	how much/how many
	ordinal/cardinal numbers	

7 Working With English Learners Who Have Experienced Trauma

Yosef moved with his family to a large city in the southeastern United States. He and his family are Somali Bantu refugees from southern Somalia who speak Af Maay. Yosef's family is relieved to be in America, a country that they heard had no violence, something that they escaped after a lifetime of persecution. Within their first weeks of moving to the country, Yosef begins a full-day kindergarten program with Mrs. Marsh, an experienced teacher who has successfully taught immigrant children from Mexico and the Caribbean. Her class is warm and welcoming to new learners of English. She speaks Spanish but has had little experience with children from Somalia, especially the persecuted Bantu.

On the first day of school, the class goes out to the playground after lunch. In order to line students up at the end of recess to return to their classes, playground aides blow loud whistles to signal the end of the outdoor play. When the children come back to the classroom, Mrs. Marsh asks where Yosef is. He is subsequently found on the playground crouched under a bench. He is obviously frightened, and Mrs. Marsh thinks that maybe one of the older children bullied him. Upon questioning her students and the playground aides, Mrs. Marsh can find no reason for his fright. Since Yosef can't express himself in English, he is unable to tell her why he hid under the bench.

Emmanuel and his mother watched his father, brother, and sisters perish in the earthquake in Port-au-Prince, Haiti. For several days after the earthquake, he and his mother wandered through their community in shock while helplessly sifting through the devastating rubble in search of friends and extended family. After living for a year in a temporary structure provided by the Red Cross, Emmanuel and his mother moved to Massachusetts with the help of distant relatives. Emmanuel enrolled in a middle school where was given a test that determined that he was an English learner (EL) at the beginning level and was placed in a sheltered immersion program in which he would work with teachers who have been trained to teach him English and subject matter content.

When Emmanuel starts Mr. Hickson's social studies class, the teacher motions for him to sit near a Haitian peer. Mr. Hickson knows how important it is for Emmanuel to be near a peer who is from the same country and who speaks Creole, his home language. Shortly after the beginning of class, a fire drill bell rings. When Emmanuel hears the loud blaring sound, it is eerily similar to what he experienced in Haiti. Even though his peer attempts to tell him that it is a drill and not a real fire event, Emmanuel is terrified and begins to shake uncontrollably. He then runs out of the school onto the city's streets, finds the subway to his home, and, once there, refuses to return to school.

Pedro and his mother moved from a village in Puebla, Mexico, to New York City. They do not have documented status to live in the United States. His mother has avoided enrolling in any of the community-based public programs for which she and Pedro would be eligible. They exist as quietly as possible so as not to arouse any suspicion from others. They also have no connections to anyone in their Latino cultural community. To obtain enough money for housing and food, Pedro's mother works over 55 hours a week in below-minimum-wage jobs where her immigration status is not questioned. While they are happy to be living in New York City, his mother's chronic fears of deportation are a constant source of stress for them. Similar to many undocumented parents, while Pedro's mother has come to the United States in search of a better life—including a good education for her son—her chronic fear, economic worries, and feelings of isolation have had a significant impact on her and her son. In school, Pedro cries easily and avoids actively engaging with others. His teacher finds it difficult to bring Pedro out of his shell.

Creating classrooms for beginning learners of English involves more than creating spaces for English and content learning. Teachers must consider the reality that many ELs come from families that have experienced significant trauma and violence. According to the Family Violence Prevention Fund, women and children represent 66% of the total population of immigrants and many have experienced violence of various types, including domestic, and trauma in their lives (Isserlis, 2000). In addition, chronic stress is an important factor among the nation's children, and it is well documented in relation to a particular population. Over 5.5 million children are being reared by parents who are living in the United States without legal documentation (Passel & Cohn, 2012; Yoshikawa, 2011). While our nation often engages in a political debate about undocumented immigrants, we often do not think of its impact on a child's well-being or development. In a study about the influence of undocumented status on child development, it was found that young children of undocumented parents were much less likely to be enrolled in early education and care settings. These families also had fewer social ties to their cultural community, fewer resources, and far fewer benefits to improve their child's develpoment (Yoshikawa, 2011). It was also found that these parents were much less likely to obtain a driver's license, credit card, and savings and checking accounts or resources requiring identification such as food stamps, housing, and child care subsidies. Parents were also much more likely to work many more hours than other groups of people and were far more likely to work below minimum wage. Many live in constant fear of deportation, financial turmoil, and isolation. The level of psychological distress among the nation's unauthorized population cannot be minimized.

While the issue of trauma is something that many teachers are aware of, we might not think of its prevalence with beginning learners of English because we are so concerned with helping them learn English. If we do not prepare ourselves for the realities of our EL population, we may unwittingly ignore some of the crucial needs of ELs that have experienced or are experiencing violence and trauma.

Going back to one of the cases at the beginning of this chapter, Yosef and his family experienced significant trauma and violence in their home country. While the blowing of a whistle may seem innocuous to many, the practice should make us think carefully about what should occur in schools to make children feel safe and welcome. This is especially important for students who are not able to express themselves in English or articulate why the routine activities that are occurring are so troubling for them.

WHAT DO WE MEAN BY TRAUMA?

Yosef, Emmanuel, and Pedro have experienced psychological trauma and distress. Their reactions to their learning environments are a reflection of their unique individual and subjective responses. Unfortunately, these responses prohibit them from participating in the learning process. Responses such as these may be due to the trauma of experiencing war or civil strife, such as Yosef did; natural disasters, such as Emmanuel did; or personal trauma or violence, such as Sofia did. Students who have experienced trauma or violence may become withdrawn, noncompliant, poorly motivated, and/or have little persistence to complete or even attempt to engage in the learning process. It is difficult for teachers to understand the influence of violence when students' English is limited and they cannot express their fears. It is also difficult for teachers to differentiate between reactions to violence and typical culture shock. In both cases a student may become withdrawn, as Pedro is. Many ELs and their families experience significant trauma and violence and are at high risk of responding to the learning environment with these behaviors. So, what do we mean by trauma?

Trauma is an individual's psychological response to a threatening event or series of threatening events (Craig, 2008; Giller, 1999; Terr, 1991). Yosef's traumatic response to the whistle on the playground was quite different than his classmates' response. Similarly, Emmanuel's response to the school's fire drill and Pedro's high level of introversion are also distinct from others in their classes. These three examples illustrate individual traumatic responses to events and are typical of beginning ELs who have experienced trauma. What they have in common is that the events they experience in school evoke a traumatic memory, a specific fear, and a specific individual response to that perceived fear (Craig, 2008; Giller, 1999). Students who have experienced or are living with trauma and/or violence react differently to situations, and not all of them experience psychological trauma. Trauma can and does have a deep and prolonged effect on some students' ability to cope emotionally, physically, and cognitively (Giller, 1999). It can also impact brain development in a myriad of ways, including "language, attention, executive functioning, emotional and behavioral regulation, memory, and/or relationships" (Cole, 2008, p. ix).

One of the more widely known researchers on childhood trauma is Lenore Terr. Terr (1991) describes different types of trauma from a single to a series of repeated events, including natural disasters (e.g., hurricane, earthquake), technological disasters (e.g., car or plane crash), and criminally violent events such as child abuse and neglect. Through her research, Terr found that children who experience repeated trauma and violence are more likely to experience difficulties psychologically over a prolonged period of time, including their school-age years.

HOW PREVALENT ARE TRAUMA AND VIOLENCE?

Unfortunately, trauma and violence are occurring in epidemic proportions for many school-age children, including ELs (Craig, 2008; Groves, 2002; Osofsky & Osofsky, 1999). For beginning ELs, this is particularly true because so many are refugees coming from war-torn countries. In 2009, for example, 74,654 refugees arrived in the United States, with the largest groups coming from Afghanistan, Iraq, Somalia, and Sudan. Others include survivors of natural disasters, such as the earthquake in Haiti and the earthquake and tsunami in Japan. Further, immigrants have moved to the United States from countries that are also experiencing civil strife. In addition, a significant number of immigrants are undocumented and experience very high levels of chronic stress from fear of deportation, living in poverty, and being isolated (Yoshikawa, 2011). Hence, many children who have experienced or are experiencing trauma and violence are represented in the general and EL student populations, and we must be prepared for this reality in our schools and classrooms. It should be noted that beginning ELs who suffer trauma would not have the language to express their fear. It is up to teachers to anticipate the fears that their students might have.

WHAT STEPS ARE IMPORTANT TO TAKE?

Creating an environment that is sensitive to the needs of ELs who have experienced trauma and violence should include four important components, drawing from the work of Craig (2008) and Yoshikawa (2011):

1. An empathetic approach

2. The means for collaboratively working with students to ensure that they feel safe, trusted, and welcome

3. Policies and routines that parallel students' needs

4. Support in accessing public community-based programming and services that are targeted to the needs of this population

In addition, we must acknowledge that caring for students who have experienced powerful trauma and violence in their lives can be quite taxing on us as teachers. It is therefore important to be proactive by acknowledging this fact:

5. We are likely to need assistance in supporting our students, and this aid will help us cope and avoid becoming overwhelmed and, as a result, burnt out.

Using an Empathetic Approach

Let's return to the case of Yosef. When Mrs. Marsh realized, after researching Yosef's background, that the whistle was much too troubling to him, she felt very badly for what had occurred. The more she learned about Yosef's background, the more sympathetic she became. For example, she observed that he rarely played with anyone at recess. She thought it would make Yosef happy if he stayed in the classroom during recess and became her helper. When she implemented this plan, she believed that he seemed happy to stay in the classroom. An important question that Mrs. Marsh should think about, however, is how her plan limited his capacity to socialize and interact with his classmates.

Being too sympathetic can thwart our efforts to help our students learn how to self-regulate (Craig, 2008). While it is important for us to create a welcoming and secure environment, it can be challenging not to overcare for our students. By this, we mean that it can be difficult not to take on all of their problems and challenges as our own. Being too sympathetic may prevent us from supporting students in learning how to manage their own behaviors. Supporting our students in ways that help them regulate their own behaviors is critically important.

Typical behavioral plans that are used with the general population are not targeted specifically for students such as Yosef who have experienced trauma or violence (Craig, 2008). Rather, they are plans that expect students to be able to control their behaviors and tolerate frustration (Craig, 2008). Let's look a little more closely at the reasons why a typical behavioral plan might not be successful. Children living in trauma have had little control over their lives. Either a single powerful event or a series of events has occurred or is occurring that is totally out of their control or management. Therefore, they do not have the internal self-management skills from which to draw. They need to learn these in a safe and supportive way. Here is where empathy plays an important role. It requires that teachers not punish students for behaviors that they have no real control over, including defiance. But it also requires that teachers think more carefully about the sensitive and positive ways that can be more responsive for students.

While Mrs. Marsh acted sympathetically, she must take a more asset-based stance for the sake of Yosef becoming a member of the classroom community. To do this, it might be more helpful for her to assist him in becoming an active participant at recess by going with him and helping him engage in activities that he seems to enjoy. It also is important for these types of activities to occur repeatedly so that Yosef will practice them repeatedly and have the opportunity to begin to self-regulate. The goal of empathy is to support children as they manage new activities and to continue to support them until they are able to do these activities on their own. This type of gradual release of support is essential.

Collaborating With Students and Others to Create a Safe and Secure Learning Environment

Students who suffer from psychological trauma are driven by fear of something happening that is out of their control. Imagine how fearful a situation this is for the many students who experience a memory that triggers such a powerful response. An important step is for teachers to create a safe and supportive environment by observing students carefully and trying to be proactive about keeping the classroom relaxed and enjoyable. To create a safe and welcoming classroom environment, ELs who have experienced trauma must trust that the teacher is going to care for and support them. This requires a continually nurturing environment that they can count on as being relaxed, safe, and secure.

With beginning ELs, it is important to secure as much information about them as possible in order to be able to develop the type of *trauma-sensitive* classroom that is needed. Craig (2008) refers to this as a collaborative partnership that must occur between the teacher and the student. However, unless the teacher speaks the student's home language and has depth of understanding about the student's home culture, the task of forming this safe and secure collaborative partnership may be overwhelming. This is why we recommend a bilingual bicultural teacher, assistant, translator, or other professional or support staff member to help teachers. With this support, it is much more possible to plan and implement a safe and secure classroom.

Developing and Implementing Routines and Practices That Reflect Students' Needs

Systematic and explicit instruction targeted to the developmental age and English proficiency level of all ELs is important. It is especially important for beginning ELs, as they are not yet able to grasp most of what is occurring in an English-speaking classroom. Students suffering from psychological trauma often have not had consistent experiences in their lives. If these inconsistencies occurred during early development, they can result in students needing depth of intentional instruction in sequencing, following multiple steps, understanding routines, and other behaviors that can help students feel safe and secure in their learning environment. Predictability cannot be underscored enough with beginning ELs who are experiencing or have experienced trauma and violence. It is important to initially parcel routines into small segments that ELs can follow and do sucessfully and repeat these so that students begin to gain control over their learning environment (Kilgore & Vignaly, 2011). A helpful means for thinking about this is to separate tasks into discrete single steps.

Using the same routines and practices (e.g., starting a class with a review of a unit's overarching learning objectives and the day's content and language objectives, singing a song, taking attendance) allows students to be more in control. For example, in the case of Emmanuel, for Mr. Hickson to move to a more trauma-sensitive practice, he and others at the school would have to think carefully about how to prepare students, including beginning ELs who have experienced trauma and violence, for a fire drill. It might also require that they think outside the box about what they are used to doing. Information about fire drills can be included in translated material that is given to parents. A school might decide to engage students in a practice of the drill without the shrill bell ringing. The school might also prepare its ELs by having them engage in a mock drill with a speaker of their home language. There are many ideas for helping schools create more sensitive practices. A key component, however, is for schools and teachers to develop and practice policies, including student codes of conduct, and routines that take careful account of ELs who have experienced trauma and violence. This means that schools should carefully examine their existing policies and practices and evaluate whether these are sensitive to their students.

Supporting Families in Accessing Community-Based Programming and Services

Many families of ELs are not familiar with the range of public programming and services that are available in their communities. This might include such essential programs as the Special Supplemental Nutrition Program for Women, Infants, and Children (WIC), Head Start, public preschool, afterschool programming, child care, public health, housing, legal aid, and other services. Accessing these can be particularly problematic for children of undocumented immigrants (Yoshikawa, 2011). Schools can play an important, if not essential, role in helping children and their families obtain much-needed community-based supports and benefits.

We cannot assume that parents understand how to access these supports and feel safe in doing so. In addition, we cannot assume that immigrant parents of ELs are documented (Yoshikawa, 2011). While we might not think of ourselves as outreach workers, helping families access community supports and benefits is essential for our students' well-being and development (Yoshikawa, 2011).

Supporting families in accessing community-based programming and services should be a priority. A means for doing this is to engage school guidance and adjustment counselors, outreach workers, nurses, and other stakeholders with community-based service agents and faith-based organizations. A goal of these collaborative efforts should be twofold: (1) to deepen our collective awareness about the specific needs of our EL family populations, including their health, well-being, and means for active participation in their school and home communities, and (2) to create the infrastructures needed for families to easily access community-based services and resources.

Getting Help to Support English Learners With Psychological Trauma

Working with beginning learners of English can be exciting and highly rewarding. There is nothing more special than helping students become active learners and participants in their class and school community. Supporting beginning ELs who are experiencing psychological trauma can feel like a very tall order for even the most seasoned of teachers. We need collaborative support in order to do this work well. Important components of the types of collaboration that are needed include supporting teachers' work, teachers' well being, and a professional development program.

Support for teachers' work with ELs who experience trauma and violence is needed from a mental health professional, such as clinical social worker or a psychologist, and is a critical component for working with this group of students. It can help teachers to make sense from and plan more appropriately for their students. But an important caveat must be made about this element: It is critical that these mental health professionals have training themselves in working with ELs. An absence of such training can lead to inappropriate practices being recommended.

Supports for teachers' well-being includes stress management. It is important for schools and teachers to know that working with students who have experienced trauma and/or violence can lead to developing compassion fatigue or burnout (Craig, 2008). Judie relates to compassion fatigue because she suffered from it when she worked with Haitian students in an inner-city school in her first teaching job. She didn't realize that this was the problem until Debbie explained the burnout disorder 20 years later. Judie explained that it wasn't really related to war or natural disaster but to the extreme poverty and domestic violence in the homes of her students. These children lacked warm clothing and food. Many were not in the country legally, and their parents were afraid to apply for services. Many lived with distant relatives and had left their siblings and parents behind in Haiti. Judie found that she had no support from the administration for the special needs of her students and was overwhelmed by the work. After 6 years, she left this teaching situation to work in a suburban school district. Collaborative school supports from a mental health professional can greatly help to support teachers in this powerful work in a safe and positive manner.

Professional development is also a critical component. Many teachers have not had formal training to work with beginning ELs and/or ELs who have experienced significant trauma and violence. It is important to provide professional development on (a) working with beginning learners of English; (b) using an empathetic approach; (c) collaboratively working with students to ensure that they feel safe, trusted, and welcome; and (d) designing and using consistent and routine policies and practices.

SUMMARY

In this chapter we discussed ELs who have experienced trauma (e.g., war, natural disasters, personal trauma) and how schools can develop trauma-sensitive practices while supporting social, language and literacy, academic, and thinking skill development within a whole school–whole classroom context. We discussed the following:

- what is meant by the terms *violence* and *trauma*
- a rationale for understanding the significance of trauma and violence as it relates to teaching beginning ELs
- using an empathetic approach
- the purpose of using a collaborative approach among school personnel
- the critical importance of creating policies and routines that parallel students' needs
- the type of professional development that is needed to successfully work with this population

Since many beginning ELs who have experienced violence and trauma have also had limited or no formal education, we will continue to develop our discussion of high-quality classroom environments for beginning EL in Chapter 8, which is devoted to a very important segment of the EL population. In Chapter 8, we will discuss how schools can develop an instructional model for students with limited or interrupted formal educations. And we will continue to use an asset-based model by focusing on strengths and capacities as they relate to beginning learners of English.

8 Teaching English Learners With Limited or Interrupted Formal Education

Marie-Louise is a seventh-grade English learner (EL) who came to northeastern Massachusetts from Léogâne, Haiti, after the 2010 earthquake that displaced thousands of families. Prior to the earthquake, Marie-Louise attended school sporadically. Her school was poorly funded, with 50 students in a class and few materials. Lesson were written on a chalkboard and read chorally by the students, who copied the information on paper. Although Marie-Louise attended school when she could when it was open, the school was closed for 8 months after the earthquake. A distant relative helped her family move from Haiti to the United States and to enroll Mary-Louise in the local school district. She does not possess literacy skills in her primary language or the academic development of her U.S. peers.

Saffia is a 14-year-old Liberian student who came to the United States and enrolled as a freshman in a high school near Kansas City, Missouri. He has never been to school, held a pencil, or read or written in any language. Saffia's first language is Krahn, and he also speaks English but not the formal English used in Liberian schools. He uses informal, Creole English. Saffia was chosen by his family to be the child that they would support to go to school in the United States and earn a high school diploma. School is very difficult for him. He struggles socially and is greatly challenged academically, especially with abstract concepts.

Pedro is a seventh-grade EL. His father has been a migrant worker in various regions of the United States for a number of years. They move to be near where there is work. During the winter months they have lived in southern Texas and Southern California, and in the spring they have often made their way to the northeastern region of the county to plant fruits and vegetables. Recently, his father heard that there is work in the fishing and meatpacking industry, and the family is looking to move closer to where the work is located. Pedro has attended well over 20 schools and has never lived in any one place long enough to have completed one school year. While he has attended school, his educational experiences have been limited. Many of these experiences have been negative, with teachers often feeling frustrated with his lack of preparedness and Pedro feeling as frustrated at the prospect of starting over again in an educational system that is not fluid and with peers who are always new.

In this chapter, we address how schools can develop an instructional model for students with limited or interrupted formal education (SLIFE). A popular term that is used in much of the research is SIFE, referring to students with interrupted formal education. In this book we are using SLIFE as it includes students with limited formal education. In general SLIFE or SIFE are defined as students who are entering U.S. schools after second grade who function at least 2 years below grade level in reading and math (Advocates for Children of New York, 2010).

Using an asset-based model, we focus on the advantages of using project-based learning and other collaborative methods with this student population.

DIFFERENT CHARACTERISTICS AMONG STUDENTS WITH LIMITED OR INTERRUPTED FORMAL EDUCATION

To begin our discussion, let's look at the different characteristics used to describe ELs who do not possess literacy skills in either their home or second language. In Chapter 2, we discussed the continuum of prior literacy experiences among ELs. We showed how orientation toward time, collectivism, and literacy behaviors affect success in school. We also discussed the reality that the majority of ELs live in poverty and how this affects some students' access to the resources that they need in order to learn. In Chapter 7, we showed how trauma affects the education of ELs. In this chapter we bring all of these elements together. Why? Many students with limited or interrupted formal education are from families with no or limited literacy experiences, live in poverty, and have experienced trauma and violence in their lives. Within this spectrum are three groups that reflect SLIFE who are also beginning learners of English. These include ELs who have

- been subjected to interrupted education because of natural disasters, political unrest, war, or migration (e.g., Saffia);
- experienced interrupted schooling due to lack of educational opportunities or poor schooling in their home countries (e.g., Marie-Louise); and/or
- attended school for the same number of years as their U.S. peers, but their school attendance has been significantly disrupted by migration or the poor quality of schooling in their home country (e.g., Pedro).

The first type of SLIFE includes those students whose education has been interrupted by civil war, natural disasters, and other conditions that have limited their formal educations. Saffia has never attended school at all. He comes from Liberia, a country that experienced civil war, which interrupted his education for 14 years. In addition, there were very few public schools in the rural area of Liberia where Saffia lived.

The second kind of SLIFE come to this country having experienced conditions that made consistent school attendance impossible. They arrive as refugees and enter school without any or with very limited educational experiences. As we noticed in Marie-Louise's scenario, not only did she came from a very poor school in Haiti with limited resources, but also the traumatic event of an earthquake significantly interrupted her education.

The third group of SLIFE migrates from one community to another due to a myriad of reasons, including following the migrant work and trying to find affordable housing. They also often come to school without the same prior educational experiences as their peers. Students from this group have had a sporadic educational experience and come to school with learning needs that are distinct from their peers (Calderón, 2007, DeCapua & Marshall, 2010; Freeman & Freeman, 2002).

DIFFERENT LEARNING NEEDS

ELs with these experiences require explicit instruction and multiple opportunities to see how literacy is used in a variety of settings, such as reading the newspaper, recipes, or sports, as well as how literacy is used for different academic purposes (Burt, Peyton, & Adams, 2003). They also need an empathetic approach to learning.

What is particularly challenging for SLIFE is that they may feel and be put down by their peers and others for their lack of literacy skills. For example, let's look at two fourth-grade ELs: Javier, who is capable of reading a chapter book independently, and Alfredo, who has had limited literacy experiences. They are engaged in a social studies unit about the positive and negative impacts that people have had on the environment. Their teacher separates the class into small groups and engages them in a group project of reading various Internet sources on this topic and developing a poster depicting some of the positive and negative impacts that people have had on their environment. Javier is able to sift through a number of websites and determine various approaches for handling the task. He has no problem surfing the web and is adept at finding sites that are written in his primary language. Alfredo is not capable of doing this task and feels very badly that he cannot participate. ELs who have not been exposed to literacy instruction are likely to be or at least feel stigmatized (Burt et al., 2003) that they do not possess the literacy skills that they need to perform school-based tasks. An appropriate approach includes two prongs: empathy and the assignment of tasks and activities that are meaningful and have goals that can be achieved by SLIFE.

Unfortunately, many schools do not know about the needs of SLIFE and do not create instructional programming that is responsive to their needs. As a result, schooling becomes an impossible task, and many of these students turn off or disconnect from the learning process. In addition to being sensitive and empathetic to SLIFE, we must pay focused attention to their learning needs. An important first step is ascertaining as much as possible about a student's past learning experiences. Many SLIFE may not possess formal records and transcripts (Hamayan, Marler, Sanchez-Lopez, & Damico, 2007), but it is still important to gather information about their prior learning experiences. Interviewing students and their families is a helpful and essential means of understanding the background experiences of SLIFE and, in particular, whether they had the opportunity to develop the literacy skills that they need to be successful in school. The next section details some important factors that should be considered when developing programming for EL and in determining who might come from SLIFE backgrounds.

THE PRIOR SCHOOLING EXPERIENCES OF AN ENGLISH LEARNER

In Chapter 3, we provided an interview process that should be held for every enrolling EL (see Resource 3.4). It included a series of questions dealing with topics such as the length of time that the student attended school, the language of instruction, and a description of the prior schooling experiences, including the length of the school day and daily schedule. When educators learn that a student might have had interrupted or no formal education, an additional series of questions should be asked. These may be found in Resource 8.1. The purpose of these interview questions is to secure as much information about the student, his or her prior schooling, interests, and purposes for attending school. It is important to create programming that is based on and drawn from the information gathered from the interview and initial assessment process. That way the programming addresses the student's English proficiency level; literacy level; prior personal, cultural, and world experiences; and academic learning experiences, if any. School districts need to find bilingual translators who speak the same language as the incoming students and their families. In Saffia's case it could be difficult to find someone who speaks his first language, Krahn. We suggest contacting reliable community members to help.

BUILDING PROGRAMMING FOR SLIFE WHO ARE ALSO BEGINNING LEARNERS OF ENGLISH

An important first step for designing instructional programming for SLIFE is to determine whether there is a critical mass of them. Interventions must be applied to address the needs of SLIFE, but it is important to ascertain whether this must be done on a programmatic level for a large number of SLIFE or, in the case of schools with very small numbers of these students, on an individual level. While many believe that older students who are enrolling in U.S. public and public charter schools for the first time need specific programming to develop basic literacy and numeracy skills, younger learners would benefit from this as well. A good method for determining who should receive this type of programming is to consider the grade levels in which literacy is expected. We believe that students from the third grade forward benefit from receiving an instructional program that is targeted for the specific needs of SLIFE and that it might be considered for second-grade students as well.

WHAT DO SLIFE NEED?

Beginning ELs with limited or interrupted formal education need a program of instruction that is distinct from ELs who are fully literate, as they do not have the literacy behaviors and background experiences from which to draw. ELs with limited or interrupted formal educational experiences need time to catch up with their peers and to develop basic literacy and numeracy skills. They need explicit instruction to learn what it means to be a member of a classroom and school community (Ariza, 2006; DeCapua & Marshall, 2011; Hamayan et al., 2007). The time required to do this is quite distinct from the time needed to help beginning ELs who possess literacy skills and behaviors in their first language. Students who come to school with limited or no formal educations should be expected to require and be given more time to close the academic language and content/subject matter learning gap (e.g., literacy, numeracy). But what is the best means for accomplishing this important goal?

A DIFFERENT APPROACH TO LEARNING

Earlier in this book, we discussed the importance of having school-matched literacy and academic skills. This could not be truer for SLIFE. American educators focus on developing independent learners who can think abstractly, and they feel that students should be individually accountable for their learning (DeCapua & Marshall, 2011; Rogoff, 2003). Students who have had limited or interrupted formal education frequently come from countries that are not industrialized and where education has been informal. They have important and quality knowledge about everyday life and concrete information about what they need to know for the near future.

Another factor that greatly affects these students is that they often come from collectivist cultures. As we discussed in Chapter 2, people from collectivist cultures focus on relationships within the group. They are concerned about their responsibilities to that group. The needs of the group supersede the needs of the individual members. This is directly opposed to the individualistic cultures of Western countries, where students are encouraged to become independent and succeed individually.

DeCapua and Marshall (2011) call this difference *cultural dissonance*, and it can lead to isolation, high dropout rates, and academic failure for SLIFE. They list three major hurdles that SLIFE encounter in U.S. schools:

1. SLIFE are collectivist, pragmatic, and oral in their traditions, in direct contrast to mainstream U.S. culture.

2. Reading and writing are challenging to SLIFE, as these are often new activities for them.

3. The individualist and academic orientation of schools in the United States presents an overwhelming culture clash.

Unfortunately, much of what we have observed in practice is that school communities often treat SLIFE as empty vessels that need knowledge "poured in." Yet when their prior learning experiences are valued as rich funds of knowledge (Gonzalez, Moll, & Amanti, 2005), it can greatly help shift the focus from what students do not have to what is greatly possible. To do this requires that we support creating and delivering lessons that are relevant to our students' lives and building strong connections between the content that is to be learned and our students prior personal, cultural, and world knowledge. Let's look at what Mrs. Jefferson does to help her student, Alberto, learn.

Alberto grew up in Central America, where he worked with his uncle, a bus driver. From a young age, Alberto was put in in charge of collecting money and providing change as well as issuing bus tickets. When he moved from Central America to the United States at the age of 11, he enrolled in school for the first time. When school personnel learned that Alberto had never attended school, they assumed that he had no academic skills. As luck would have it for Alberto, Mrs. Jefferson is a native speaker of Spanish and took time to learn about his life experiences. When she learned about his prior work experience, she was able to tap into it. She remarked, "He is really smart in math. I just needed to build my program around what he already had." What did Mrs. Jefferson do?

She understood that Alberto's primary form of communication was oral. She understood that this mode needed to be her primary form of instruction along with connecting her educational goals and objectives with his prior life experiences. This is a core concept for SLIFE. Teachers should focus on oral transmission of information, as it is generally a primary mode of communication that SLIFE possess (DeCapua & Marshall, 2011). Mrs. Jefferson also knew that Alberto would benefit from learning experiences in which he could communicate in the language of content with his peers. This called for her to use cooperative learning, including paired and small-group work. In addition, she knew that the tasks that she created for Alberto had to be directly connected to his prior experiences; they had to be pragmatic. Indeed, cooperative grouping of students and pragmatic activities are critical features of instructional programming for SLIFE so that information is presented in a meaningful and familiar manner (De Capua & Marshall, 2011). Mrs. Jefferson also created project-based classroom experiences that mimicked Alberto's prior experiences. For example, one such activity involved creating a restaurant experience in which Alberto was the cashier. Teaching strategies for all SLIFE need to include hands-on and visual approaches that we usually associate with real-life, authentic situations.

Programming for SLIFE, as seen in Figure 8.1, must address differences between SLIFE and the general student population. Drawing from DeCapua and Marshall (2011), these elements are also foundational:

1. Accept that SLIFE learn in a different way. It is critical to gather information about these students' prior learning in order to build an instructional program that is fundamentally based on continuous connections to students' prior personal, cultural, and world knowledge.

2. Introduce academic learning by making connections to what students know.

3. Provide support so that students will fully transition to programming with the general EL population.

Figure 8.1 Comparison of Learning for SLIFE and General Education Students in U.S. Schools

Characteristics of Learning for SLIFE	Characteristics of Learning for General Education Students
Information is immediately relevant. Students learn in cooperative groups. Cooperation and sharing is encouraged. Responsibility for learning is collective. Information is transmitted orally.	Information has relevance at some point in the future. Students learn independently. Competition is encouraged. Responsibility for learning is individual. Information is transmitted through writing.

Source: Adapted from DeCapua & Marshall (2011).

INSTRUCTIONAL PROGRAMMING FOR SLIFE

Freeman and Freeman (2002) provide us with a framework for better ensuring the success of SLIFE. While their framework is intended for older learners, we believe that it is essential and should be used with SLIFE from the third grade forward. By the end of the second grade, many traditional students are able to read and take on literacy independently. Conversely, SLIFE have not had the time needed to develop these essential literacy skills and behaviors. They need an educational program that pays particular and focused attention to the steps outlined in Figure 8.2. When there is a critical mass of students, it can be very helpful to create programming specifically for them. When there is not, it is important to create an individual instructional plan that is targeted for the same purpose.

STUDENT ENGAGEMENT

Helping SLIFE become invested in learning requires that we understand what constitutes meaningful instruction. Connecting curriculum to socially relevant issues that are personal to students, especially SLIFE, provides an important means for helping them become invested in learning (Vasquez, 2010). One way to think about this is to consider the importance of creating theme-based units of study and connecting them to issues that are personal

Figure 8.2 Keys for School Success for SLIFE

1. Engage students in challenging, theme-based curriculum with language modifications to develop academic concepts.

2. Draw on students' background—their experiences, cultures, and oral language traditions.

3. Organize collaborative activities and pragmatic tasks; scaffold or shelter instruction to build students' academic English proficiency.

4. Create culturally relevant content to develop confident students who value school and themselves as learners. Use information that is immediately relevant.

Source: Adapted from Freeman & Freeman (2002).

to students. Georgia Garcia and Heriberto Godina (2004) and Ofelia Garcia (1999) discuss the importance of theme-based units of study and how it helps students become more knowledgeable about the content to be learned. Take, for example, a fourth-grade math unit whose goal is for students to be able to express whole numbers as fractions and recognize fractional equivalents of whole numbers. While the unit of study is drawn from the Common Core State Standards (2011), how teachers of beginning-level ELs who are SLIFE make it meaningful and understandable has to be distinct from what would occur for students who have developed literacy skills in their native language and have school-matched grade-level academic backgrounds. Teachers need to develop lessons that recognize the pragmatic, collectivist, and oral language traditions of SLIFE and focus on what is immediately relevent to them. Then they can move to the more academic orientation of U.S. education using scaffolding to help students learn to read and write.

DEVELOPING PROGRAMS FOR SLIFE

Getting back to one of the scenarios at the beginning of the chapter, Saffia had no former schooling. He has instructional needs that go far beyond the average English as a second language (ESL) class. Many high schools are developing programs that are designed just for SLIFE so that they can be taught basic literacy. SLIFE who have recently come to the United States don't fit into English language arts programs designed specifically for ELs in which students read modified versions of *Romeo and Juliet*. They are also not helped much by ESL programs that are designed for literacy-oriented beginning ELs. They will not do well in ESL programs where they are mixed with intermediate or advanced ELs. SLIFE need programs that teach basic reading and life skills. They need programs that are specially designed for their English language development needs.

In Chapter 4 we discussed newcomer programs, which Short and Boyson (2012) define as "specialized academic environments that serve newly arrived, immigrant English language learners for a limited period of time" (Executive Summary, p. 1). In our opinion, a specialized program such as those provided by newcomer high schools as well as programs for third and as early as second grade students that help SLIFE catch up to peers is an excellent way to apply the methods cited by DeCapua and Marshall (2011). Not only do these programs provide English language and basic literacy instruction, they provide necessary backing and information about social services, making connections with parents and the broader school community.

DRAWING ON STUDENTS' BACKGROUNDS

All learners' benefit from an educational program that is grounded in their prior experiences. This could not be truer for SLIFE. It is critical to take the time needed to learn about their prior learning experiences, to expect these to be distinct from those of peers with literacy and grade-level academic skills, and to design and deliver instruction that draws from the background experiences of SLIFE. Let's go back to Alberto and look at a mathematics unit that is being taught. His math teacher wants to know about his prior math experience. She is not sure where to begin, so she asks Alberto, in Spanish, if he knows how to tell time and how to count money. When she asks the second question, his eyes light up and he smiles. He tells his teacher that one of his favorite activities in El Salvador was to sell bus tickets and collect fares on his uncle's bus. This information is extremely helpful to his teacher. She begins to think about the possibilities of designing a unit of study on fractions that will be based on Alberto's prior experience. As she considers the possibilities, she learns that El Salvador uses the same monetary system as the United States. She begins to see various possibilities for making this unit of study both interesting and compelling and connected to the assets that Alberto brings to the classroom. This is extremely important for SLIFE. They need to see that the information they are learning in school is immediately relevant to their lives (DeCapua & Marshall, 2011).

USING A COLLABORATIVE LEARNING PROCESS TO BUILD ACADEMIC SKILLS

As we said in Chapter 6, building educational programming that is connected to students' personal, cultural, language, and world experiences is as important as using a collaborative learning process that includes paired and group work (Ruiz-de-Velasco, Fix, & Clewell, 2000; Short & Boyson, 2012). Not only is this an important method; it also takes a good deal of thought in order to make a space in which ELs with no or limited formal education can flourish. Helping them feel and be valued and honored as rich resources is imperative (DeCapua & Marshall, 2011; Freeman & Freeman, 2002; Zacarian, 2011).

Indeed, creating such programming should be foundational in any classrooms with SLIFE. Paired and small-group spaces provide opportunities for SLIFE to use, apply, and learn the language of content. However, we also know that paired and group work are complex endeavors and that teachers of SLIFE must create spaces in which all students feel safe and welcome. For example, many ELs, especially beginning learners of English who are also SLIFE, may not feel comfortable speaking in front of peers who are not like them. An important method of addressing this complex problem is to build an instructional program that is drawn from the assets of SLIFE. For example, Pedro's teacher designed and delivered a mathematics unit of study that was targeted to the learning goal of creating a poster that depicted various types of travelers on a bus, including adults who paid full fare, seniors who paid half fare, and children under 5 years old who paid a quarter fare. The type of tasks that she created for this unit of study drew from Pedro's expertise and promoted him as an asset in her class. SLIFE will have more success in classrooms when projects and activities are assigned in groups and when topics are immediately relevant and have an oral language component.

CREATE CULTURALLY RELEVANT CONTENT TO DEVELOP CONFIDENT STUDENTS WHO VALUE SCHOOL AND THEMSELVES AS LEARNERS

ELs with no or limited formal schooling experiences need to feel and be valued by their peers and teachers. They also need to see materials that are specifically targeted to meet their needs. Securing materials that depict students' native cultures and background experiences should be a step in the planning and delivery of instruction. For example, beginning learners of English should be able to recognize words and phrases through contextual supports. This requires that instructional materials be provided to illustrate and depict what it is that we want them to learn. Because beginning ELs who are also SLIFE may be silent during this period of time (Fairbairn & Jones-Vo, 2010), graphic organizers and visual, audio, and kinesthetic supports, such as movies, music, dancing, and drawing, are critical. These are also critical for promoting reading and writing instruction that leads to literacy development and enhancement.

SUMMARY

In this chapter, we discussed the different kinds of students identified as SLIFE. Based on the research and experience of DeCapua and Marshall (2011), we suggested that educators incorporate these major components into their lessons for SLIFE:

- Instruction needs to be immediately relevant and interconnected.
- Students should work in collaborative groups, and oral traditions should be recognized when designing lessons.
- Teachers need to recognize that education in the United States is individualistically oriented toward the future and dependent on the written word. They must find ways to balance the two points of view in their instruction of SLIFE.

In Chapter 9, we will discuss how professional development for teachers can help school districts develop effective instruction for beginning ELs.

RESOURCE 8.1
Interview of Parent/Guardian and/or Newly Identified English Learner With Limited, Interrupted, or No Prior Formal Education

Newly identified English learners with limited, interrupted, or no prior formal education and/or their parents/guardians should be interviewed to assist in building an effective instructional SLIFE program. The following questions are intended for this purpose. The interview may be conducted with parents/guardians, parents/guardians and their child, or with the student. The person conducting the interview should complete this form.

Date of Interview: _____

Student Name: _____ Grade: _____

SLIFE Interviewer:_____ Position:_____

Who was interviewed: (parent/guardian ☐ parent/guardian with student ☐ student ☐)

1. How often was school in session?

2. How often was your child able to attend school when it was in session?

3. Did anything prevent your child from attending school regularly?

4. What subjects were taught in your child's previous school?

5. What was expected of your child in school?

6. What do you believe is critical for this school to know about your child?

7. What are some of the key goals and objectives that you and your child have for school?

9 Providing Effective Professional Development

Mr. Santiago has a variety of roles and responsibilities as the principal of an urban high school. One is creating a professional development plan to strengthen the academic performance of the students in his school. To begin the task of determining the type of professional development that is needed, he looks at his students' scores on state assessments. He sees that the students who are performing below benchmark levels are the English learners (ELs) in his school. This reality makes him think about the types of professional development that have occurred and whether they have been tailored for the teachers and staff in his school.

As Mr. Santiago reviews the past 5 years of professional development, including some on differentiating instruction, he realizes that none has been specifically targeted to ELs. He begins to think about what should be included in the professional development plans for ELs. What should Mr. Santiago do?

WHAT SHOULD BE INCLUDED IN HIGH-QUALITY PROFESSIONAL DEVELOPMENT?

There are various forms of professional development study, ranging from college courses to mini-workshops. Professional development for in-service teachers can range from a few hours to a one-day event, a series of workshops to a multi-day off-site national conference activity and more.

College course work for pre- and in-service teachers typically includes a type of sustained study that the National Staff Development Council advocates. The National Staff Development Council defines effective professional development as including "a comprehensive, sustained, and intensive approach to improving teachers' and principals' effectiveness in raising student achievement" (Learning Forward, 2012, para. 1). This definition is a helpful springboard for this chapter as well as for principals, such as Mr. Santiago and others, who wish to implement professional development as part of their school or district plan for educators and educational leaders of ELs. It is also helpful for higher education institutions that are preparing educators and educational leaders. The following factors, though different, are important consider:

- ELs are the "fastest growing segment of the preK–12 student population" (Short & Boyson, 2012, p. 1).
- ELs have been challenged much more than the general population to perform successfully in and graduate from school (Short & Boyson, 2012).
- U.S. Census data indicates that over half of the nation's ELs attend schools where they represent less than 1% of the student population (National Center for Education Statistics, 2004).
- Most teachers and administrators have not had much in the way of formal training to teach this population (Hollins & Guzman, 2005; Ladson-Billings, 1995).

Taking these factors into account, we believe that it is essential to provide professional development study that is targeted for beginning learners of English. This is especially important for schools with low numbers of ELs or preservice teachers who will work in these contexts, as we have found them to be much less prepared for this student population. Teaching beginning ELs requires a very different approach than teaching ELs who possess an intermediate or higher level of English proficiency. In Chapter 1, we referred to beginning-level ELs as those who come from countries and commonwealths outside of the continental United States and have no prior experience in English as well as U.S.-born ELs who are entering school for the first time and are at the beginning stages of English language development.

Many teachers and administrators believe that the beginning stage is limited to a period of a few months. For example, during a recent professional development session, one teacher's comment was emblematic of the group's beliefs about beginning learners of English: "It's already March; how is it possible that students who came in September are still beginners?"

We stated in Chapter 1 that most beginning learners will take at least 1 year to develop more advanced levels of English. For many, however, including students with limited or interrupted formal education and/or students who have experienced trauma and violence, it may take longer. A critical element for students' success is a school's preparedness to meet their needs. Professional development is a critical means for ensuring this preparedness. In addition to the study of theories and practices related to working with this population, we believe professional development should include three important authentically based activities: observing, reflecting, and interviewing.

OBSERVATIONAL ACTIVITIES

According to Calderón and Minaya-Rowe (2011), there are many complexities to providing high-quality professional development for educators of ELs. Some of these include the range of professional preparedness, from preservice educators enrolled in teacher education programs to veterans with years of experience and knowledge to new teachers just starting out in their respective educational field. Observational protocols have been identified as a helpful means of understanding the practice of teaching as well as what is working and what needs strengthening (Calderón & Minaya-Rowe, 2011; Echevarria, Vogt, & Short, 2008). Many teachers, including one of us, have used these extensively to help support the study of the profession as well as the effectiveness of their work to improve or strengthen student performance, to make data-driven decisions, develop classroom instruction, and increase parent–school engagement (Zacarian, 2011). In addition, the nationally known ExC-ELL Observation Protocol (Calderón & Minaya-Rowe, 2011) and Sheltered Instruction Observation Protocol (Echevarria et al., 2008) make extensive use of these tools.

REFLECTION ACTIVITIES

Self-reflection and collaborative reflection activities also strengthen the practice of teaching ELs. They greatly help us connect what we are learning with our personal experiences and our collective understanding about the student populations with whom we are working (Moll, Amanti, & Gonzalez, 1992). Reflection includes understanding something from various points of view and perspectives as well as the assumptions that we hold about it (Loughran, 2002). Two types of reflection are considering what we experience in the moment (and teaching requires us to make many on-the-spot, moment-to-moment actions) and thinking back to something that we did or experienced (Schön, 1987). Both of these types are critical for educators, especially in contexts in which there is collaborative dialogue (Wade, Fauske, & Thompson, 2008). We believe strongly in the importance of a reflective stance. It can greatly help veteran and novice teachers and school leaders, as well as preservice teachers and administrators, develop more of a much-needed comprehensive approach to working with ELs.

INTERVIEWING ACTIVITIES

In addition to observation and reflection activities, interviews are also a very helpful means of understanding student, parent, and school populations. We believe that interview activities are a fine complement to professional development. They provide us with the means to collect data, understand different perspectives, and, importantly, learn how to ask questions that help yield the most significant information that is needed to strengthen our individual and collective thinking about working with ELs. This is an especially helpful activity for understanding and developing ways to effectively teach ELs (Janzen, 2008).

COLLABORATIVE PROFESSIONAL DEVELOPMENT GROUPS

Collaboration and collegiality are important dimensions of professional growth. We believe that professional development, in institutions of higher education and public and public charter school settings, should be

- a collective responsibility,
- based on rigor and aligned with state standards,
- a well-prepared opportunity for professional growth,
- a consistent and routinized event that occurs on a regular basis, and
- an opportunity for teams to analyze data and make data driven decisions. (Learning Forward, 2012)

WHY IS BOOK STUDY AN IMPORTANT FORMAT?

We believe that book study gives educators the opportunity to collectively explore a topic of study using a collegial process for a professional "our-o-logue" (Zacarian, 2013). Here is what we mean by an our-o-logue: In practice, professional development might be delivered by a teacher educator in a higher education institution, an expert coming in to a district, or educators attending a conference to listen to an expert. It may also be in the form of a leader guiding a group in its professional development work. The first might be named a my-o-logue, in which a teacher educator or expert has some important information to share with a group of learners. The second might be named a dialogic activity, implying that the conversation moves from one all-knowing authority to another or is in the form of a dyad or di-o-logue. An our-o-logue is one in which the group is creating a common language, knowledge, and way of thinking and acting. According to Donohue, Van Tassel, and Patterson (1996) and Zacarian (1996), book study is a useful method when there is a need to examine change and/or when diverse perspectives are needed. Book study, using an our-o-logue format, in which everyone is considered a rich contributor, is ripe with possibilities for professional growth. To do this well, a whole class, such as a college classroom, should be separated into small learning groups of four to six members. In school settings, the same should occur.

STRUCTURE FOR PROFESSIONAL BOOK STUDY GROUPS

Book study meetings should be planned to occur on a regular basis, with time allocated between meetings for each member to read assigned chapters and explore these in the context using observation, reflection, and/or interview activities. In the case of the college classroom, it is very helpful to include time for students to regularly visit actual schools and classrooms in order to engage in the activities. For professional development as an in-service activity, it is equally important to schedule a series of meetings to strengthen sustainability, with time between meetings for some or all three of the activities. Here are some key roles and activities for book study groups. Each small group participants should include a group facilitator and timekeeper. Both roles are necessary so that the group facilitator can focus on (1) the structure of the group meetings, (2) group process and product, and (3) the dialogic flow (Zacarian, 1996). The role of facilitator may rotate among members or may be fulfilled by the same person throughout the study. The timekeeper role is necessary in group meetings to ensure that the group's work occurs on schedule. We also recommend that observations, interviews, and self-reflection activities be created to support the content being studied in each chapter and an authentic examination of what is being studied. To do this successfully, we recommend that the facilitator's tasks include those listed in Box 9.1. Note that the facilitator is not the leader of the group, nor is he or she the expert. Rather, the facilitator's purpose is to support an our-o-logue.

BOX 9.1　The Facilitator's Tasks

Pre-Meeting Activities

- Identifying chapter focus questions and observational tasks
- Scheduling a kickoff organizational meeting to discuss the book study structure and calendar for group meetings as well as to determine the length and schedule for each meeting
- Ensuring that the group knows the chapter, chapter focus questions, and chapter observational task assignments and due date for each

During-Meeting Activities

- Helping the group stay focused on its collective task by guiding the group forward and keeping the collective discussion flowing
- Ensuring that each member has a voice and that every participant listens to others
- Assigning a timekeeper to ensure that the meetings flows smoothly

Conclusion/Meeting Wrap-Up Activities

- Creating a review of the group process (e.g., what went well, what needs strengthening)
- Creating a review of group product (e.g., what was learned by observing and reading the chapter)
- Determining how this will be applied to actual work and assessed for its effectiveness

Figure 9.1 provides a proposed cycle for book study activities (adapted from Donohue et al., 1996). It is intended for use in a college course or in-service program. We provide a 90-minute schedule of activities for each book study meeting. The time can be adjusted up or down as needed.

At the back of this chapter (pages 116–126), we provide specific book study resources including *focus questions* and *reflection, interview*, and *observation* tasks for each chapter of our book. Resource 9.1, for example, has been specifically designed for Chapter 1 of our book, Resource 9.2 for Chapter 2, and so forth. Our intent is to provide a practical and informative means for engaging in a professional development experience that is focused on beginning learners of English.

Figure 9.1 Cycle for Book Study

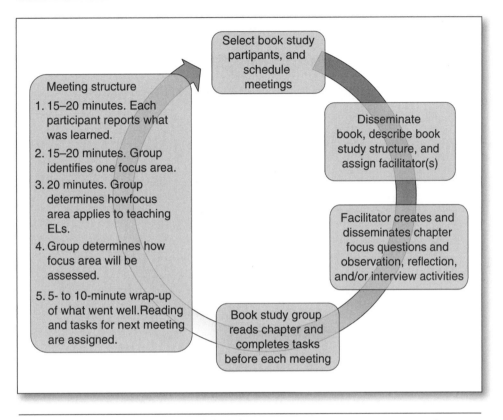

Source: Adapted from Donohue et al. (1996).

SUMMARY

In this chapter, we discussed the importance of professional development for educators of beginning-level ELs. We described effective professional development as including a comprehensive, sustained, and intensive approach. We explained how book study supports this effort and provided chapter-by-chapter guidance for using this method with our book.

Educating beginning ELs requires that we understand this dynamic population from a variety of perspectives and that we learn effective practices for working with this richly diverse group of students. When this occurs, we can build welcoming and high-quality classroom, school, and family engagement environments where ELs and their families are engaged and can flourish.

RESOURCE 9.1
Chapter 1: Seeing the Big Picture

Focus Questions to Be Discussed During Professional Book Study

1. How are ELs doing in school at a national level?

2. What are some of the reasons for this outcome?

3. Define a beginning-level EL.

Reflection Tasks

Respond to the following questions:

1. Do you speak a language other than English? If yes, what is your proficiency level in that language on a scale of 1–5 (1 being low, 5 being high)?

2. Did you learn English as a second language? If yes, please describe your experience.

3. Have you lived in a country or commonwealth other than the continental United States where the language of instruction was other than English? If yes, please describe.

4. Have you had any formal education in teaching English?

Resource Figure 9.1a Observational Tasks

Observational Tasks

1. Select a beginning EL and a time during the school day when you will observe him or her. (This might be during class or social time.) Using the protocol provided here, observe the ways in which the student is or is not included in the community.

2. Place a checkmark in each box that is relevant to your observation.

3. Use the Observation Notes section to describe observations.

Student Name: _____ Grade: _____

Observation Date: _____

Subject Matter or Social Situation Observed: _____

Student interaction	Student listens and receives information from staff and/or peers	Student has some differentiated instruction or peers accommodate his or her English language level	Staff or peer and student share the effort to learn the task	Student is well supported to learn the task and staff and/or peers help student build capacity for future learning
With peers				
With teacher and other adults				
In small groups				

Observation Notes

RESOURCE 9.2
Chapter 2: Taking a Closer Look

Focus Questions to Be Discussed During Professional Book Study

1. What one sentence from the chapter resonated the most for you?

2. How did the chapter inform your beliefs about literacy?

3. How did the chapter inform your knowledge about differing beliefs about time?

4. How did the chapter inform your beliefs about the culture of collectivism and the culture of time in your thinking about education?

Interview Task

Interview a classroom teacher regarding the population of students that he or she teaches. Ask the teacher to describe the learning challenges that students experience in relation to literacy.

Reflection Tasks

Compare the interview responses with what you read in Chapter 2. How do the challenges that the teacher shared reflect or not reflect what you read?

What literacy practices should occur in school for students with (and/or being reared in families with) no or limited formal literacy education? How do these differ from what is already occurring?

RESOURCE 9.3
Chapter 3: Effective Programming for English Learners

Focus Questions to Be Discussed During
Professional Book Study

1. How do parent/student interviews help us build effective programming?

2. Why do you believe that identification assessments are key for building programs? Why are they often not enough for building programming?

Interview Task

Review the home language survey and testing that was done to identify the student as an EL. Using Resource 3.4, interview a parent and/or a student. Note what you learn from the interview that is distinct from the testing and home language survey.

Reflection Task

Compare the interview responses with what you read in Chapter 2. How do the challenges that the teacher shared reflect or not reflect what you read?

RESOURCE 9.4
Chapter 4: Selecting Models of Instruction

**Focus Questions to Be Discussed During
Professional Book Study**

1. What are some of the language instructional models used for beginning ELs?

2. Identify some of the productive tensions/challenges that are associated with the models that you have identified.

3. What models do you think would be the most challenging to implement in your particular context? Why?

4. What model do you think would work best/most effectively with beginning-level ELs? Why?

Interview Task

Meet with a teacher or administrator in a school with ELs. Ask him or her to describe in as much detail as possible the language programming that ELs receive and to discuss the challenges that they experience with the programming.

Reflection Task

Review the model descriptions included in Chapter 4. Are any of the models the ones that were described during the interview? How are they different from or the same as the challenges that are described in the chapter? What changes do you think would be helpful for this school to consider?

RESOURCE 9.5
Chapter 5: Strengthening Family–School Engagement

Focus Questions to Be Discussed During Professional Book Study

1. What are some of the key barriers to family engagement?

2. What are some key activities that schools can do to engage families?

3. Why is it important to engage families in social activities before academic activities?

Reflection Task

Review the chapter and your observations (see Resource Figure 9.5a on page 122). How were parents included or not included in this event? What might have occurred to help support active engagement?

Resource Figure 9.5a Observational Tasks

Observational Tasks

1. Attend a parent event at school. Using the protocol included here, observe the ways in which parents/guardians and/or other family members of ELs, such as grandparents, do or do not actively participate.

2. Place a checkmark in each box that is relevant to your observation.

3. Use the Observation Notes section to describe observations.

Event Type: _____

Observation Date: _____

Situation Observed: _____

Family interaction	Family listens and receives information from staff and/or peers	Family has some differentiated explanation or peers who support understanding	Staff or peers and family share the effort to learn the activity	Families are well supported to learn the activity (e.g., parent conference) and staff and/or peers help parents build capacity for future activities like this one
With peers				
With teacher and other adults				
In small groups				

Observation Notes

RESOURCE 9.6
Chapter 6: Teaching Beginners

Focus Questions to Be Discussed During Professional Book Study

1. What is culture shock, and what are the stages of culture shock?

2. What methods of instruction of beginning ELs resonated with you most?

3. Why is it important to differentiate instruction for beginning ELs?

Reflection Tasks

1. Review the chapter and your observations (see Resource Figure 9.6a on page 124). Did the EL you observed receive differentiated instruction? What might have occurred to help support the learning?

2. Which teaching strategy for differentiating instruction for ELs resonated with you most?

Resource Figure 9.6a Observational Tasks

Observational Tasks

1. Using the protocol included here, observe a beginning EL in a content area class.

2. Place a check mark in each box that is relevant to your observation.

3. Use the Observation Notes section to describe your observations.

Event Type: _____

Observation Date: _____

Situation Observed: _____

Student comprehension of lesson	Student does not receive any differentiated instruction	Student has some differentiated activities or native language support	Teacher differentiates lesson specifically for ELs	Teacher and peers participate in differentiation throughout the lesson
Student does not follow the lesson				
Student follows some of the lesson				
Student engages in the lesson				

Observation Notes

RESOURCE 9.7
**Chapter 7: Working With English Learners Who
Have Experienced Trauma**

Focus Questions to Be Discussed During Professional Book Study

1. What do we mean by trauma? What are the different types of trauma that an EL might experience?

2. What steps are important to take when a child is experiencing trauma?

Interview Task

Interview a school social worker, guidance counselor, or school psychologist. Ask the following questions:

1. What are the typical types of trauma experienced by the general school population?

2. What types of trauma do you see in ELs? Is there an increase in the amount of trauma among ELs?

3. What does the school do when it recognizes that a student has suffered from trauma?

Reflection Task

Review the chapter and the results of your interview. How does the information in the chapter compare with the information from the interview?

RESOURCE 9.8
Chapter 8: Teaching English Learners With Limited or Interrupted Formal Education

Focus Questions to Be Discussed During Professional Book Study

1. Name the different types of students with limited or interrupted formal education (SLIFE).

2. How did the chapter inform your knowledge about SLIFE?

Interview Task

Interview a classroom or subject area teacher regarding the SLIFE that he or she teaches. Ask the teacher to describe the learning and social challenges that these students experience in relation to content area work.

Reflection Task

Reflect on what program would best meet the needs of the SLIFE in your school.

References

Advocates for Children of New York. (2010). *Students with interrupted formal education: A challenge for New York City Public Schools*. New York, NY: Author. Retrieved from http://www.advocatesforchildren.org/sites/default/files/library/sife_2010.pdf

Ariza, E. N. W. (2006). *Not for ESOL teachers: What every classroom teacher needs to know about the linguistically, culturally, and ethnically diverse student*. New York, NY: Pearson.

August, D., & Shanahan, T. (Eds.) (2006). *Executive summary: Developing literacy in second-language learners: Report of the National Literacy Panel on Language-Minority Children and Youth*. Mahwah, NJ: Lawrence Erlbaum.

Board of Regents of the University of Wisconsin System. (2011). *WIDA's ELD standards, 2012 edition*. Retrieved from http://www.wida.us/standards/elp.aspx

Brown, H. D. (1994). *Principles of language learning and teaching*. Englewood Cliffs, NJ: Prentice Hall.

Burt, M., Peyton, J. K., & Adams, R. (2003). *Reading and adult English language learners: A review of the research*. Washington, DC: Center for Applied Linguistics. Retrieved from http://eric.ed.gov/ERICWebPortal/contentdelivery/servlet/ERICServlet?accno=ED505537

Calderón, M. (2007). *Teaching reading to English language learners, grades 6–12: A framework for improving achievement in the content areas*. Thousand Oaks, CA: Corwin.

Calderón, M. E., & Minaya-Rowe, L. (2011). *Preventing long-term ELs: Transforming schools to meet core standards*. Thousand Oaks, CA: Corwin.

Capps, R., Fix, M., Murray, J., Ost, J., Passel, J., & Herwantoro, S. (2005). *The new demography of America's schools: Immigration and the No Child Left Behind Act*. Washington, DC: Urban Institute.

Center for Applied Linguistics. (1999). *Two-way bilingual education programs in practice: A national and local perspective*. Retrieved from http://www.cal.org/resources/digest/ed379915.html

Cole, S. (2008). Foreword. In S. E. Craig, *Reaching and teaching children who hurt: Strategies for your classroom* (pp. ix–xii). Baltimore, MD: Paul H. Brookes.

Collier, V. P., & Thomas, W. P. (2009). *Educating English learners for a transformed world*. Albuquerque, NM: Fuente Press.

Common Core State Standard Initiative. (2011). *Mathematics, grade 3, number and operations—fractions*. Retrieved from http://www.corestandards.org/the-standards/mathematics/grade-3/number-and-operations-fractions/

Craig, S. (2008). *Reaching and teaching children who hurt: Strategies for your classroom.* Baltimore, MD: Paul H. Brookes.

Crawford, S. (2011, December 3) The new digital divide. *The New York Times.* Retrieved from http://www.nytimes.com/

Cummins, J. (2001). *Language, power, and pedagogy.* Bristol, UK: Multilingual Matters.

DeCapua, A., & Marshall, H. W. (2010). Serving ELLs with limited or interrupted education: Intervention that works. *TESOL Journal, 1,* 49–70.

DeCapua, A., & Marshall, H. W. (2011). *Breaking new ground: Teaching students with limited or interrupted formal education in U.S. secondary schools.* Ann Arbor: University of Michigan Press.

Denny, K. (2002). New methods for comparing literacy across populations: Insights from the measurement of poverty. *Journal of the Statistical Society, Series A (Statistics in Society), 165,* 481–493. Retrieved from http://www.jstor.org/action/showPublication?journalCode=jroyastatsocise3

A distinct population. (2009). *Quality Counts, 28*(17), 15.

Donohue, Z., Van Tassel, M. A., & Patterson, L. (Eds.). (1996). *Research in the classroom: Talk, texts, and inquiry.* Newark, DE: International Reading Association.

Duke, K., & Mabbot, A. (2001). An alternative model for novice-level elementary ESL education. *WITESOL Journal, 17,* 11–30.

Echevarria, J., Vogt, M., & Short, D. J. (2004). *Making content comprehensible for English learners: The SIOP model* (2nd ed.). Boston, MA: Allyn & Bacon.

Echevarria, J., Vogt, M. E., & Short, D. J. (2008). *Making content comprehensible for English learners: The SIOP model* (3rd ed.). Boston, MA: Allyn & Bacon.

Egbert, J. L., & Ernst-Slavit, G. (2010). *Access to academics: Planning instruction for K–12 classrooms with ELLs.* Boston, MA: Allyn & Bacon.

Fairbairn, S. V., & Jones-Vo, S. (2010). *Differentiating instruction and assessment for English language learners: A guide for K–12 teachers.* Philadelphia, PA: Caslon.

Ferlazzo, L. (2011). Involvement or engagement? *Educational Leadership, 68*(8), 10–14.

Frankenberg, E., Siegel-Hawley, G., & Wang, J. (2010). *Choice without equity: Charter school segregation and the need for civil right standards.* Los Angeles: University of California, Los Angeles, Civil Rights Project/Proyecto Direchos Civiles. Retrieved from http://civilrightsproject.ucla.edu/research/k-12-education/integration-and-diversity/choice-without-equity-2009-report/frankenberg-choices-without-equity-2010.pdf

Freeman, Y. S., & Freeman, D. E. (2002). *Closing the achievement gap: How to reach limited-formal-schooling and long-term English learners.* Portsmouth, NH: Heinneman.

Gándara, P. (2010). Overcoming triple segregation: Latino students often face language, cultural, and economic isolation. *Educational Leadership, 68*(3), 60–65.

Garcia, E. E. (2005). *Teaching and learning in two languages.* New York, NY: Teacher's College Press.

Garcia, E. E., Jensen, B. T., & Scribner, K. P. (2009). The democratic imperative. *Educational Leadership, 66*(7), 8–13.

Garcia, G. E., & Godina, H. (2004). Addressing the literacy needs of adolescent English language learners. In T. Jetton & J. Dole (Eds.), *Adolescent literacy: Research and practice* (pp. 304–320). New York, NY: Guildford Press.

Garcia, O. (1999). Educating Latino high school students with little formal schooling. In C. J. Faltis & P. Wolfe (Eds.), *So much to say: Adolescents, bilingualism, and& ESL in the secondary school* (pp. 61–82). New York, NY: Teachers College Press.

Gersten, R., & Woodward, J. (1995). A longitudinal study of transitional and immersion bilingual education programs in one district. *Elementary School Journal, 95,* 223–239.

Gibbons, P. (2009). *English learners, academic literacy, and thinking: Learning in the challenge zone.* Portsmouth, NH: Heinemann.

Giller, E. (1999). *What is psychological trauma?* Retrieved from http://www.sidran .org/sub.cfm?contentID=88&sectionid=4

Goldenberg, C., & Coleman, R. (2010). *Promoting academic achievement among English learners: A guide to the research.* Thousand Oaks, CA. Corwin.

Gonzalez, N., Moll, L. C., & Amanti, C. (2005). *Funds of knowledge: Theorizing practices in households, communities, and classrooms.* Mahwah, NJ: Lawrence Erlbaum.

Gottlieb, M., Katz, A., & Ernst-Slavit, G. (2009). Paper to practice: Using the English language proficiency standards in preK–12 classrooms. Alexandria, VA: Teachers of English to Speakers of Other Languages.

Groves, B. M. (2002). *Children who see too much.* Boston, MA: Beacon Press.

Hall, M. T. (1983). *The dance of life: The other dimensions of time.* New York, NY: Doubleday.

Hall, E. T. (1990). *The hidden dimension.* New York, NY: Knopf Doubleday.

Hamayan, E., Marler, B, Sanchez-Lopez, C., & Damico, J. (2007). *Special education considerations for English language learners: Delivering a continuum of services.* Philadelphia, PA: Caslon.

Haynes, J. (2005a). ESL = Essential student learning. *Essential Teacher, 2*(1), 6–7.

Haynes, J. (2005b). *Getting started with English language learners: How educators can meet the challenge.* Alexandria, VA: Association for Supervision and Curriculum Development.

Haynes, J. (2007a). Can two teachers be better than one? *Essential Teacher, 4*(3), 6–7.

Haynes, J. (2007b). *Getting started with English learners: How educators can meet the challenge.* Alexandria, VA: Association for Supervision and Curriculum Development.

Haynes, J. (2008). Out of the storage room. *Essential Teacher, 5*(2), 6–7.

Haynes, J., & Zacarian, D. (2010). *Teaching English language learners across the content areas.* Alexandria, VA: Association for Supervision and Curriculum Development.

Hays, J. (2009). *Japanese mothers and housewives: Having children, duties, education and school lunches.* Retrieved from http://factsanddetails.com/japan.php?item id=625&catid=18

Henderson, A. T., Mapp, K. L., Johnson, V. R., & Davies, D. (2007). *Beyond the bake sale: The essential guide to family-school partnerships.* New York, NY: New Press.

Honawar, V. (2009). Training gets boost. *Quality Counts, 28*(17). Retrieved from http://www.edweek.org/

Hollins, E., & Guzman, M. T. (2005). Research on preparing teachers for diverse populations. In M. Cochran Smith & K. M. Zeichner (Eds.), *Studying teacher education: The report of the AERA Panel on Research and Teacher Education* (pp. 477–548). Mahwah, NJ: Lawrence Erlbaum.

Honigsfeld, A., & Dove, M. (2010). *Collaboration and co-teaching: Strategies for English learners.* Thousand Oaks, CA: Corwin.

Hyerle, D., Curtis, S., & Alpert, L. (Eds.). (2004). *Student successes with using thinking maps: School-based research, results, and models for achievement using visual tools.* Thousand Oaks, CA: Corwin.

Isserlis, J. (2000). *Trauma and the adult English language learner.* Retrieved from http://www.cal.org/caela/printer.php?printRefURL=http%3A//www.cal.org/caela/esl_resources/digests/trauma2.html

Janzen, J. (2008). Teaching English language learners in the content areas. *Review of Educational Research, 78,* 1010–1038.

Kilgore, J., & Vignaly, J. (2011, May). *Culturally and linguistically diverse students and trauma.* Presentation at the Massachusetts English Learner Leadership Council Conference, Leominster, MA.

Krashen, S. (1985). *The input hypothesis: Issues and implications.* New York, NY: Longman.

Krashen, S. (1989). *Language acquisition and language education.* Englewood Cliffs, NJ: Prentice Hall.

Krathwohl, D. R., Bloom, B. S., & Masia, B. B. (1973). *Taxonomy of educational objectives, the classification of educational goals. Handbook II: Affective Domain.* New York, NY: David McKay.

Ladson-Billings, G. (1995). Multicultural teacher education: Research, practice and policy. In J. A. Banks & C. A. McGee Banks (Eds.), *Handbook of research on multicultural education* (pp. 747–761). New York, NY: Macmillan.

Lawrence-Lightfoot, S. (2003). *The essential conversation: What parents and teachers can learn from each other.* New York, NY: Random House.

Learning Forward. (2012). *Definition of professional development.* Retrieved from http://www.learningforward.org/standfor/definition.cfm

Lindholm-Leary, K. (2001). *Dual language education.* Avon, UK: Multilingual Matters.

Loughran, J. J. (2002). Effective reflective practice: In search of meaning in learning about teaching. *Journal of Teacher Education, 53,* 33–43.

McClure, G., & Cahnmann-Taylor, M. (2010). Pushing back against push-in: ESOL teacher resistance and the complexities of coteaching. *TESOL Journal, 1.* 121–129.

Moll, L., Amanti, C., Neff, D., & Gonzalez, N. (1992). Funds of knowledge for teaching: Using a qualitative approach to connect homes and classrooms. *Theory Into Practice, 31,* 132–141

National Center for Education Statistics. (2004). *English language learners in U.S. public schools: 1994 and 2000.* Retrieved from http://nces.ed.gov/pubsearch/pubsinfo.asp?pubid=2004035

National Center for Education Statistics. (2009). *Number and percentage of children ages 5–17 who spoke only English at home, who spoke a language other than English at home and who spoke English with difficulty, and percent enrolled in school: Selected years, 1980–2009.* Retrieved from http://nces.ed.gov/programs/coe/tables/table-lsm-1.asp

National Writing Project. (2009). *Literacy, ELL, and digital storytelling: 21st century learning in action.* Retrieved from http://www.nwp.org/cs/public/print/resource/2790

Office for Civil Rights (2005). Questions and answers on the rights of Limited English Proficient students. Retrieved July 4, 2012: http://www2.ed.gov/about/offices/list/ocr/qa-ell.html

Osofsky, J. D., & Osofsky, H. J. (1999). Developmental implications of violence in youth. In M. Levine, W. B. Carey, & A. C. Crocker (Eds.), *Developmental and beavhioral pediatrics* (3rd ed., pp. 493–498). Philadelphia, PA: Saunders.

Passel, J., & Cohn, D. (2012). *U.S. foreign-born population: How much change from 2009 to 2010?* Washington, DC: Pew Hispanic Center. Retrieved from http://www.pewhispanic.org/files/2012/01/Foreign-Born-Population.pdf

Pransky, K. (2008). *Beneath the surface: The hidden realities of teaching culturally and linguistically diverse young learners, K–6.* Portsmouth, NH: Heinemann.

Pransky, K. (2009). There's more to see. *Educational Leadership, 66*(7), 74–78.

Ravitch, D. (2011). *The death and life of the great American school system: How testing and choice are undermining education.* New York, NY: Basic Books.

Rogoff, B. (1990). *Apprenticeship in thinking: Cognitive development in social context.* New York, NY: Oxford University Press.

Rogoff, B. (2003). *The cultural nature of human development.* New York, NY: Oxford University Press.

Ruiz-de-Velasco, J., Fix, M. E., & Clewell, B. C. (2000). *Overlooked and underserved: Immigrant students in U.S. secondary schools.* Retrieved from http://www.urban.org/publications/310022.html

Schmidt, M. A. (2000). Teacher's attitudes toward ESL students and programs. In S. E. Wade (Ed.), *Inclusive education: A casebook and readings for prospective and practicing teachers* (pp. 109–116). Mahwah, NJ: Lawrence Erlbaum.

Schön, D. A. (1987). *Educating the reflective practioner.* San Francisco, CA: Jossey-Bass.

Short, D. J., & Boyson, B. A. (2012). *Helping newcomer students succeed in secondary school and beyond.* Washington, DC: Center for Applied Linguistics.

Soltero, S. (2004). *Dual language learners: Teaching and learning in two languages.* New York, NY: Pearson.

Teachers of English to Speakers of Other Languages. (1996–2007). *PreK–12 English language proficiency standards framework.* Retrieved from http://www.tesol.org/s_tesol/sec_document.asp?CID=281&DID=13323

Terr, L. (1991). Childhood traumas: An outline and overview. *American Journal of Psychiatry, 148,* 10–20.

U.S. Department of Education. (2004). *Title IX—General provisions.* Retrieved from http://www2.ed.gov/policy/elsec/leg/esea02/pg107.html

U.S. Department of Education, Office of Civil Rights. (1991). *Policy update on schools' obligations toward national origin minority students with limited-English proficiency.* Retrieved from http://www2.ed.gov/about/offices/list/ocr/docs/lau1991.html

U.S. Department of Education.(October 6, 2011). Statement of U.S. Secretary of Education Arne Duncan on the passing of Civil Rights Leader Fred Shuttlesworth. Retrieved July 4, 2012: http://www.ed.gov/news/press-releases/statement-us-secretary-education-arne-duncan-passing-civil-rights-leader-fred-sh

Valdes, G. (2001). *Learning and not learning English: Latino students in American schools.* New York, NY: Teachers College Press.

Vasquez, V. (2010). *Getting beyond "I like the book": Creating space for critical literacy in K–6 classrooms* (2nd ed.). Newark, DE: International Reading Association.

Wade, S. E., Fauske, J. R., & Thompson, A. (2008). Prospective teachers' problem solving in online peer-led dialogues. *American Educational Research Journal, 45,* 398–442.

Wiggins, G., & McTighe, J. (2005). *Understanding by design* (Expanded 2nd ed.). Alexandria, VA: Association for Supervision and Curriculum Development.

Yoshikawa, H. (2011). *Immigrants raising citizens: Undocumented parents and their young children.* New York, NY: Russell Sage Foundation.

Yoshikawa, H. (2012, May). *Immigrants raising citizens: Undocumented parents and their young children's development: knowing our students.* Presentation at the MATSOL 40th Anniversary Conference, Framingham, MA.

Zacarian, D. (1996). *Learning how to teach and design curriculum for the heterogeneous class: An ethnographic study of a task-based cooperative learning group of native English and English as a second language speakers in a graduate education course* (Doctoral dissertation). Available from ProQuest Dissertations and Theses database. (UMI No. 9639055)

Zacarian, D. (2007). Mascot or member? *Essential Teacher, 4*(3), 10–11.

Zacarian, D. (2011). *Transforming schools for English learners: A comprehensive framework for school leaders.* Thousand Oaks, CA: Corwin.

Zacarian, D. (2012). *Serving English learners: Laws, policies and regulations.* Washington, DC: Colorín Colorado. Retrieved from http://www.colorincolorado.org/pdfs/policy/ELL-Policy-Guide.pdf

Zacarian, D. (2013). *Mastering academic language: A framework for support student achievement.* Thousand Oaks, CA: Corwin.

Zeichner, K., & Hoeft, K. (1996). Teacher socialization for cultural diversity. In J. Sikula, T. Buttery, & E. Guyton (Eds.), *Handbook on research on teacher education* (2nd ed., pp. 525–547). New York, NY: Macmillan.

Index

CORWIN

A SAGE Company

The Corwin logo—a raven striding across an open book—represents the union of courage and learning. Corwin is committed to improving education for all learners by publishing books and other professional development resources for those serving the field of PreK–12 education. By providing practical, hands-on materials, Corwin continues to carry out the promise of its motto: **"Helping Educators Do Their Work Better."**